Lecture Notes in Computer Science

Lecture Notes in Artificial Intelligence   14756

Founding Editor

Jörg Siekmann

Series Editors

Randy Goebel, *University of Alberta, Edmonton, Canada*
Wolfgang Wahlster, *DFKI, Berlin, Germany*
Zhi-Hua Zhou, *Nanjing University, Nanjing, China*

The series Lecture Notes in Artificial Intelligence (LNAI) was established in 1988 as a topical subseries of LNCS devoted to artificial intelligence.

The series publishes state-of-the-art research results at a high level. As with the LNCS mother series, the mission of the series is to serve the international R & D community by providing an invaluable service, mainly focused on the publication of conference and workshop proceedings and postproceedings.

Marija Živković · Jeffrey Buckley ·
Marianna Pagkratidou · Gavin Duffy
Editors

Spatial Cognition XIII

13th International Conference, Spatial Cognition 2024
Dublin, Ireland, June 25–28, 2024
Proceedings

 Springer

Editors
Marija Živković 🆔
Technological University Dublin
Dublin, Ireland

Marianna Pagkratidou 🆔
University of Minnesota
Minneapolis, MN, USA

Jeffrey Buckley 🆔
Technological University of the Shannon:
Midlands Midwest
Athlone, Ireland

Gavin Duffy 🆔
Technological University Dublin
Dublin, Ireland

ISSN 0302-9743   ISSN 1611-3349 (electronic)
Lecture Notes in Artificial Intelligence
ISBN 978-3-031-63114-6   ISBN 978-3-031-63115-3 (eBook)
https://doi.org/10.1007/978-3-031-63115-3

LNCS Sublibrary: SL7 – Artificial Intelligence

This Springer imprint is published by the registered company Springer Nature Switzerland AG
The registered company address is: Gewerbestrasse 11, 6330 Cham, Switzerland

If disposing of this product, please recycle the paper.

Preface

Welcome to the proceedings of the 13th International Spatial Cognition Conference (SC 2024) in Dublin. This conference marked a significant gathering of minds dedicated to the exploration of spatial cognition, a field at the intersection of cognitive, developmental, and educational psychology, neuroscience, computer science, geography, and beyond.

Although established quite recently in January 2019, Technological University Dublin evolved from Institutes of Technology in Dublin that have a history dating back to 1885 with the establishment of a Technical College in Kevin Street. This was the former home of the School of Electrical & Electronic Engineering, the host of SC 2024 and coordinator of SellSTEM – 'Spatially Enhanced Learning Linked to STEM', an MSCA Innovative Training Network funded under Horizon 2020 (project no. 956124, Jan 2021 to Dec 2024). With 15 PhD students spread across 10 universities in 8 countries in Europe, SellSTEM is concerned with understanding the role of spatial ability in STEM learning, how spatial ability can be developed, both integrated with and separated from STEM learning, and how such development can be implemented in a sustainable way in the classroom. The SellSTEM network supported the hosting of SC 2024. It is worth noting that the previous iteration of the conference was held online during COVID 19 and it was a challenge to reach out to the community and bring the conference back to an in-person event.

The scope and purpose of this conference were vast, aiming to delve into the intricate mechanisms behind how humans perceive, reason about, and navigate through space. From understanding the developmental origins of spatial abilities to exploring the applications of spatial cognition in fields such as STEM learning, urban planning, and virtual reality, this conference provided a platform for interdisciplinary exchange and collaboration.

Twelve papers were submitted. The committee accepted and published nine papers. The peer review process was meticulously conducted with a double-blinded approach. Each paper was reviewed by two expert reviewers, and a third expert reviewer resolved any remaining ambiguities, ensuring that only high-quality research contributed to the discourse.

The conference took place over four days in the Central Quad, located on the Grangegorman Campus of TU Dublin, from June 25 to 28. On Day 1, four symposia were delivered in two parallel sessions, followed by a workshop. Each symposium had four papers and covered these topics: "Visual spatial perspective taking" (Brady & Kessler), "Evaluating small-scale spatial assessments" (McKee et al.), "Promoting Spatial Thinking across STEM Education Contexts" (Pagano), and "Advances in Measurement of Large-Scale Spatial Ability" (Zhou et al.). The workshop, "Many Spaces: Sharing VR Environments for Studying Navigation", was led by the esteemed Nora Newcombe and provided attendees with hands-on experience and insights into the latest advancements in the field. This interactive session was a highlight of the conference, offering practical knowledge and fostering lively discussions amongst participants.

Each of Days 2, 3, and 4 began with a keynote and was followed by paper sessions. The first keynote was delivered by Prof. David Uttal of Northwestern University, who reflected on the relation between "real" maps and "cognitive maps", how real maps present mental models of the world that people then incorporate into their cognitive maps, a long-standing debate that has recently been resurrected. This was followed by two paper sessions: "Spatial ability in Mathematics" and "Navigation". A poster session was held on the afternoon of Day 2 with 24 posters presented. Dr. Katie Gilligan Lee, Ad Astra Fellow, University College Dublin, delivered the second keynote. Her research lies at the intersection of psychology, neuroscience, and education and she has a keen interest in translating foundational findings into classroom practice. Katie is interested in understanding how spatial development relates to STEM success and in the potential of different interventions, including spatial skill training, block building, and spatial language, to enhance children's mathematics (and wider STEM) outcomes. Paper sessions on Day 3 covered "Spatial Abilities in Early Childhood" and "Spatial Ability Development through STEAM". The final keynote was delivered by Prof. Alexander Klippel of Wageningen University who discussed recent development at the interface of AI, digital twins, XR, and Blockchain, also referred to as the Metaverse. He presented a potential theoretical grounding of the Metaverse by framing it inspirationally in Christian Freksa's notion of strong spatial cognition. While there are multiple theoretical perspectives possible, it is postulated that strong spatial cognition has the potential for advancing a synergistic geo-science, spatial cognition, and AI perspective on the Metaverse. This keynote was followed by paper sessions on "Perception" and "Gender". In all, 24 papers were presented at the conference.

As editors of these proceedings, we are thrilled to present a compilation of the groundbreaking research and insights shared at the Spatial Cognition 2024 conference. We hope that these proceedings serve as a valuable resource for scholars and practitioners alike, inspiring further exploration and innovation in the dynamic field of spatial cognition. We would also like to thank all who helped to make the conference possible: the Steering Committee for their support and permission to host the conference, the Organising Committee for the many months of hard work, the support staff at TU Dublin, the volunteers who helped during the week and those who chaired sessions and helped in many other ways.

Warm regards,
Marija Živković
Jeffrey Buckley
Marianna Pagkratidou
Gavin Duffy

Organisation

Program Committee Chairs

Jeffrey Buckley	Technological University of the Shannon: Midlands Midwest, Ireland
David Dorran	Technological University Dublin, Ireland
Gavin Duffy (Conference Chair)	Technological University Dublin, Ireland
Petra Jansen	University of Regensburg, Germany
Günter Maresch	University of Salzburg, Austria
Colm O'Kane	Technological University Dublin, Ireland
Marianna Pagkratidou	University of Minnesota, USA
Marija Živković	Technological University Dublin, Ireland

Local Organisation Committee

David Dorran	Technological University Dublin, Ireland
Gavin Duffy	Technological University Dublin, Ireland
Nwabuogo Enwerem	Technological University Dublin, Ireland
Colm O'Kane	Technological University Dublin, Ireland
Marija Živković	Technological University Dublin, Ireland

Poster Co-chairs

Günter Maresch	University of Salzburg, Austria
Marianna Pagkratidou	University of Minnesota, USA

Steering Committee

Thomas Barkowsky (Executive Officer)	University of Bremen, Germany
Anthony G. Cohn (Chair)	University of Leeds, UK
Ruth Conroy Dalton	Northumbria University, UK
Sara I. Fabrikant	University of Zurich, Switzerland
Ken Forbus	Northwestern University, USA
Christoph Hölscher	ETH Zurich, Switzerland

| Asifa Majid | Radboud University, Netherlands |
| David Uttal | Northwestern University, USA |

Program Committee

Thomas Barkowsky	University of Bremen, Germany
Sven Bertel	University of Bremen, Germany
Stefano Borgo	Institute of Cognitive Science and Technology, Italy
Jeffrey Buckley	Technological University of the Shannon: Midlands Midwest, Ireland
Xiaoli Chen	Zhejiang University, China
Christophe Claramunt	Naval Academy Research Institute and Art & Métiers Institute of Technology, France
David Dorran	Technological University Dublin, Ireland
Inese Dudareva	University of Latvia, Latvia
Zoe Falomir	Umeå University, Sweden
Lena Gumaelius	Royal University of Technology, Sweden
Danielle Harris	University of Canberra, Australia
Marian Hickendorff	Leiden University, Netherlands
Stephen Hirtle	University of Pittsburgh, USA
Toru Ishikawa	Toyo University, Japan
Petra Jansen	University of Regensburg, Germany
Dietsje Jolles	Leiden University, Netherlands
Leo Jost	University of Regensburg, Germany
Remke Klapwijk	Delft University of Technology, Netherlands
Alexander Klippel	Wageningen University, Netherlands
Werner Kuhn	University of California, Santa Barbara, USA
Diarmaid Lane	University of Limerick, Ireland
Günter Maresch	University of Salzburg, Austria
Chiara Meneghetti	University of Padua, Italy
Debbie Mills	Bangor University, UK
Dan Montello	University of California, Santa Barbara, USA
Dace Nansome	University of Latvia, Latvia
Nora Newcombe	Temple University, USA
Colm O'Kane	Technological University Dublin, Ireland
Marianna Pagkratidou	University of Minnesota, USA
Jack Parkinson	University of Glasgow, UK
Francesca Pazzaglia	University of Padua, Italy
Jason Power	University of Limerick, Ireland
Claudia Quaiser-Pohl	University of Koblenz, Germany

Ilyse Resnick	University of Canberra, Australia
Kai-Florian Richter	Umeå University, Sweden
Angela Schwering	University of Münster, Germany
Jurgis Škilters	University of Latvia, Latvia
Sheryl Sorby	Michigan Technological University, USA
Jeroen Spandaw	Delft University of Technology, Netherlands
Maria Rosaria Stufano Melone	Polytechnic of Bari, Italy
Holly Taylor	Tufts University, USA
Thora Tenbrink	Bangor University, UK
Jennifer Thom	University of Victoria, Canada
Martin Tomko	University of Melbourne, Australia
David Uttal	Northwestern University, USA
Nico Van de Weghe	Ghent University, Belgium
Constanze Vorwerg	University of Bern, Switzerland
Valentin Vulchanov	Norwegian University of Science and Technology, Norway
Mila Vulchanova	Norwegian University of Science and Technology, Norway
Stephan Winter	University of Melbourne, Australia
Diedrich Wolter	University of Bamberg, Germany
Jiayan Zhao	Wageningen University, Netherlands

Sponsors

Contents

Early Childhood

Mathematics

Insights from Paper Folding: Spatial Visualization Processes and Their Link to Mathematics

Danielle Harris$^{(\boxtimes)}$ (iD) and Tom Lowrie (iD)

STEM Education Research Centre, University of Canberra, Canberra, Australia
danielle.harris@canberra.edu.au

Abstract. Spatial visualization (SV) involves transformations to the structure and relations of an object through a complex sequence of maneuvers. These skills are associated with mathematics performance. Research to date primarily involves analyzing psychometric measures to determine the nature of relations. Consequently, there is in a gap in knowledge around the process-based associations between SV and mathematics. In this study, 259 Grade 8 students (52.9% female) completed tests of SV and mathematics, and open-ended paper folding tasks. They were categorized as High (HS), Mid (MS), or Low (LS) spatial. HS students completed most open-ended tasks with better than average success. Although LS students did not perform as well as HS students, those who completed the more complex open-ended fold task had higher success rates than MS students, indicating the use of effective strategies, regardless of spatial skill. There were differences in student responses for diagonal- compared with straight-fold tasks. Diagonal tasks were associated with spatial skill but not with mathematics performance. HS students used successful spatial strategies for the open-ended tasks and mathematics. For MS students, there was an association between spatial tasks and word and geometry-measurement problems. There was minimal association between the open-ended spatial tasks and mathematics for LS students. The paper concludes with a discussion around the functional role of spatial visualization in mathematics and avenues for future research.

Keywords: Spatial Visualization · Paper Folding · Mathematics

1 Introduction

Spatial visualization (SV) is considered a critical spatial skill in the link between spatial reasoning and mathematics [1] and is a commonly trained skill with transfer to mathematics achievement [2]. SV is often used as a catch-all phrase for tasks that involve a complex sequence of events where the viewer needs to encode and mentally transform an object [3, 4]. Therefore, the nature of SV tasks may involve changes to the spatial relations within an object as well as structural changes to its form [5–7]. The broad categorization of SV means that the associated psychological measures can involve a range of activities [5, 7]. For example, tests may require identifying hidden components

M. Živković et al. (Eds.): Spatial Cognition 2024, LNAI 14756, pp. 3–18, 2024.
https://doi.org/10.1007/978-3-031-63115-3_1

of shapes or objects, conversions between 2D and 3D, or tasks where paper folds are represented, holes are marked on the folded paper and a viewer needs to identify the correct unfolded paper [8]. In this study, we examine paper folding [8] in assessment form and as an open-ended task as a means of exploring cognitive processes and strategies associated with SV and their links to performance in mathematics.

1.1 Relations Between Spatial Reasoning and Mathematics

Empirical research examining spatial-mathematics relations focuses primarily on correlational and training studies [2, 9]. Researchers have been able to isolate spatial skills that have significant associations with mathematics performance (e.g., [10]). However, the outcomes remain confined to psychological training studies with little impact on classroom practice [11]. Lowrie and Logan [12] demonstrated that spatial training can be embedded in classroom teaching with significant effects on mathematics understanding. The question remains about the mechanisms that facilitate this type of transfer [13]. Mix [14] described three possible ways that spatial reasoning and mathematics could relate in real-time problem-solving. The first two relate to cognitive processes, that is, either through the decoding of symbolic representations (e.g., arrangement of numbers or geometric properties) or the development of mental models that map question content in ways that support problem solving (e.g., visualizing question material and resulting changes). The third relates to concrete tools (e.g., gestures or physical representations) that can be used to offload some of the cognitive work. Mix argued that these functions can be engaged in different and complementary ways depending on the task, thereby providing avenues to examine spatial skills beyond isolated training. Understanding the cognitive processes that help students navigate tasks may provide a practical solution for building spatial skills in the context of mathematics teaching [12].

1.2 Paper Folding

The Paper Folding Test (PFT; [8]) is a classic and widely used instrument to measure SV [5]. It is one of three tests in the visualization factor developed by the Educational Testing Service (with Form Board Test and Surface Development Test [8]). When completing the PFT, participants need to identify the resulting representation after visualizing the folding and unfolding of a sheet of paper with a punched hole (Fig. 1). The test is a prototypical SV measure because it requires a complex sequence of mental manipulations to the form of an object from a fixed perspective [6]. The task is often used as an outcome measure, but rarely as a learning or process tool. Given the prevalence of SV in spatial training literature [2], in this study we explore paper folding as an incarnation of SV and its associated cognitive processes.

Paper Folding Links to Mathematics. Correlational and training studies have uncovered moderate links between the PFT and a range of mathematics content areas, with little knowledge of why they exist [9]. The skills engaged when completing the test have intrinsic links to mathematics content as well as an association through cognitive processes [14]. For example, performance on geometry and word problems are directly related to PFT performance [15].

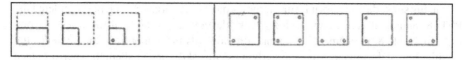

Fig. 1. Sample Paper Folding Test item from "Kit of Factor-Referenced Cognitive Tests" by Ekstrom et al. Copyright 1976 Educational Testing Service.

The spatial visualization skills engaged by the PFT support geometry by enabling students to overlay spatial processes, such as imagining or transforming objects and perspectives, onto geometric properties and relations. In both the PFT and geometry, problem-solvers need to make predictions about what will happen when changes are made to objects and their relations [16]. The PFT involves a series of prescribed steps while in geometry, transformations can occur at different scales and dimensions. In both types of tasks, spatial visualization supports problem-solving as complexity increases. Furthermore, many geometry tasks (e.g., transformations on a cartesian plane) require the same object-to-object mapping demanded by the PFT [6].

Spatial visualization supports the schematic representation of components when solving word problems [17]. The ability to encode structural relations is beneficial for success in both word problems and the PFT. For the PFT, relations are based on the positioning of holes and direction of folds and for word problems the extraction of critical structural information is key to determining correct solutions [14].

The cognitive processes elicited by paper folding tasks have explicit links with other mathematics curricula. For example, the variability and complexity of spatial maneuvers demanded by the PFT also lend themselves to the multi-step processes required in multiplicative and algebraic thinking [18].

Reflection and symmetry are central ideas within mathematics [19] and intrinsic components of the PFT [20]. The folds in the PFT items act as lines of symmetry. When a fold occurs across a diagonal line, the rules of reflection produce changes to the orientation of an array [20] or changes to the orientation of the line of reflection thereby increasing the complexity of the object-to-object mapping [6].

1.3 Context of This Study

The diverse functions of SV provide some clues as to why it is considered such a critical component in the link between spatial reasoning and mathematics [2, 9]. However, much of our understanding of this link is intuitive as research into the processes and strategies employed during spatial tasks is rare [14, 21].

Performance on the PFT provides a measure of a person's SV skills but not the way the skills are enacted [21]. The enactment of spatial skills could provide insights into the spatial visualization processes that support mathematical problem-solving. One way to explore these relations is unpacking whether the link between spatial skills and mathematics is intuitive, that is in automatic recruitment of similar strategies, or through deliberate, effortful use of spatial strategies [14]. Options to explore such strategies are possible through qualitative analysis of responses when tasks are open-ended, as opposed to the traditional multiple-choice format of assessment.

In this study data is drawn from a larger project [22]. Grade 8 students completed the PFT [8] and open-ended paper folding tasks developed and normed for this age group [23]. In Grade 8, mathematics content shifts towards the symbolic, which enables the examination of the intersection of underlying spatial skills and mathematics performance as the links are more implicit than with early mathematics [14, 16, 22].

The test manual for the PFT specifies use with students in Grades 9–16, yet the test has widespread use in school-aged populations (e.g., [22, 24, 25]). Reliability in younger cohorts is not ideal [4, 22]. Ramful [20] hypothesized that some of the issues with the measure may be due to different cognitive processes involved depending on the direction of the fold. For example, when an item involves diagonal folds, the resulting arrangement is in a different orientation compared to straight folds (either vertical or horizontal) where the orientation does not change. This challenge with non-prototypical images is common in diagonal reflection tasks among school-aged students [26]. Therefore, performance on diagonal fold items may require a level of analytical thinking in addition to spatial visualization skills [12].

Students completed open-ended, paper folding tasks as well as the PFT and mathematics measures. Three content areas of mathematics were included, geometry and word problems were identified in their links to SV by existing research, and a third number category allowed broader examination of the association with SV.

Research Questions. How do the processes, strategies and errors on an open-ended SV task inform our understanding of performance on a traditional SV test and curriculum-based mathematics assessment? How can these insights drive theories around the links between SV and mathematics?

2   Method

2.1   Participants

The 259 Grade 8 participants for this study were drawn from the larger project [22]. They ranged in age from 12 years, 6 months to 14 years, 10 months (52.9% female).

2.2   Measures and Procedure

Students completed all tasks online during the Spring Semester. Tasks were completed in classrooms within one week.

Assessment Tasks. Students completed the spatial and mathematics measures in one session. The mathematics test was presented first.

Mathematics Test. The mathematics test (Cronbach's Alpha = .82) was developed to reflect appropriate content present in the year 8 mathematics curriculum [27]. The questions were modeled on standardized assessment items and completed without the aid of a calculator. The test items were categorized according to three content areas based on curriculum guidelines: Geometry and Measurement (GM; 10 items, Cronbach's Alpha = .52), Number (6 items, Cronbach's Alpha = .58) and Word Problems (5 items, Cronbach's Alpha = .48).

Paper Folding Test. Part B of the 10-item Paper Folding Test (PFT [8]) was adapted for online testing. The test items displayed a sequence of folds executed on a piece of paper with the final image including an arrangement of holes on the folded page. Participants selected the correct arrangement of holes in the unfolded paper from a series of multiple-choice options. Students completed as many items as possible within three minutes. Each correct item was given a score of 1. Cronbach's Alpha for the PFT was .58. Part B of the PFT contains three items with straight folds only, three items with diagonal folds, and four items with a combination of straight and diagonal folds.

Open-Ended Paper Folding Tasks. Four open-ended tasks were taken from the Lohman [23] paper folding assessment. These tasks were similar in nature to the PFT but developed and normed for the sample population. Instead of students being asked to choose from multiple choice options, students were given open instructions to draw the unfolded paper however they imagined it would look. One task was given for practice with guidance from classroom teachers. The subsequent three tasks were completed individually, the focus of this paper is on these three open-ended tasks (see Table 1).

Table 1. Open-ended paper folding tasks.

#	Item	Fold direction
Task 1		Straight only
Task 2		Diagonal only
Task 3		Diagonal and straight

Task 1 involved two horizontal folds (one at a quarter and another at a half of the paper) with one punched hole. The resulting representation had three holes arranged vertically on the unfolded page. Critically, the distribution of the holes should have been represented with two in the top half of the square and one near the top of the bottom half.

Task 2 involved three diagonal folds with one punched hole. The folds occurred across three different diagonal lines and the resultant folded paper was located in the bottom right. Therefore, the unfolded arrangement would have been located across these fold lines in the bottom left corner and oriented in a rotated 2 × 2 array.

Task 3 included one diagonal fold, a vertical fold and two horizontal folds, with two punched holes. In this task, the arrangement of the pairs of holes remains the same but the number of holes are a function of correct order and position of the folds. The initial diagonal fold would have created a gap in the final folded paper resulting in an asymmetrical array of 10 holes.

2.3 Analysis

Correlations and Analysis of Variance were used for examining quantitative measures of spatial visualization (PFT) and mathematics. The open-ended task responses were drawn from student work samples, therefore much of the analysis is qualitative, with measures of association using chi-square statistics when possible and cell sizes allowed.

3 Results

In light of historical gender differences in spatial reasoning and mathematics [1], gender differences were compared for the PFT and mathematics and no significant differences were found, $F(1, 205) = 2.90, p = .09$ and $F(1, 208) = .60, p = .44$. Therefore, subsequent analysis considered all students, with no separation by gender.

3.1 Paper Folding Test

The mean for the PFT was 5.38 ($S.D. = 1.62$). To align with our three categories of open-ended tasks, the PFT items were broken down into three categories: items with only straight folds, items with only diagonal folds and items containing both straight and diagonal folds. A repeated-measures ANOVA revealed significant differences in performance based on item type, $F(2, 410) = 210.76, p < .001$, partial eta$^2 = .33$ (see Fig. 2). Students were the most successful on the items with straight folds, followed by diagonal only folds. Items containing both straight and diagonal folds had the lowest performance with students averaging less than 1 correct.

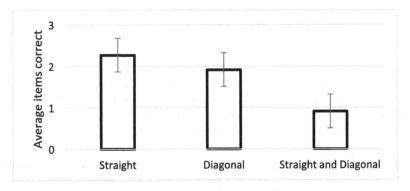

Fig. 2. Means for the three PFT categories (with error bars).

3.2 Open-Ended Paper Folding Tasks

As performance on the open-ended tasks was dichotomous (i.e., right or wrong), performance on the PFT was separated into categorical groups based on Low (LS; $N =$

56), Mid (MS; $N = 101$), and High (HS; $N = 52$) Spatial for the subsequent qualitative analysis of the paper folding tasks.

PFT performance was significantly correlated with the number of open-ended tasks correctly completed ($r = .22$, $p = .002$). Table 2 breaks down completion and success rates by spatial group. Response rates dropped off for LS and MS students across the three tasks. At the same time success rates improved for LS students across the tasks but declined for MS students. A high proportion of HS students completed all three tasks with greater than 50% success rates.

Table 2. Response and success rates on open-ended paper folding tasks.

Task 1 (straight)		Task 2 (diagonal)		Task 3 (straight and diagonal)	
Responses	Success rates	Responses	Success rates	Responses	Success rates
LS	53	30.2%	48	37.5%	39	43.6%
MS	91	48.4%	89	48.3%	68	36.8%
HS	47	51.1%	47	70.2%	40	60%

Task 1 (straight Only; Table 3). There was no significant difference in success rate based on spatial group (using Chi-square statistics), $\chi^2(2, N = 191) = 5.76, p = .056$.

Table 3. Task 1 dominant responses (percentages based on spatial group).

Spatial Group	Correct (lines)	Correct (no lines)	Error: Equal Distribution	Error: Missing Holes
LS	21%	9%	36%	19%
MS	24%	24%	26%	12%
HS	32%	19%	15%	9%

Roughly half of all students drew fold lines for Task 1, regardless of spatial skill. Of those that drew the fold lines, HS students were most likely to represent the correct fold or a partial fold while LS and MS students were more likely to divide the page into three equal parts, suggesting some difficulty with the representational system [6]. This type of representation resulted in holes equally distributed in a vertical line which conflicted with the original sequence showing the final fold clearly at half of the paper size. A greater proportion of LS and, to a lesser extent, MS students, compared with HS students used only 2 holes indicating they did not mentally represent the half-fold step.

Task 2 (Diagonal Only; Table 4). This task had a significant difference in success rate (using Chi-square statistics) based on spatial group, $\chi^2(2, N = 184) = 10.7, p =$

.005. Few LS students successfully represented the unfolded paper, roughly half of MS students were correct and 70% of HS students were correct.

For all spatial groups the greatest proportion of errors occurred when students oriented the four holes correctly but showed them in the wrong location. When students placed the holes in the wrong location, LS and MS students most often put them in the top left corner or distributed them widely around the unfolded paper. For the MS group, students were equally likely to have the holes in the wrong orientation as well (prototypical 2×2 array as opposed to a rotated array). Errors were most common amongst students who did not draw in the folds which would have clearly shown the layout and location of the holes. Only a small percentage of students represented the fold lines proportion of LS and MS students representing incorrect folds and therefore showing errors in their representation.

Table 4. Task 2 dominant responses (percentages based on spatial group).

Spatial Group	Correct (lines)	Correct (no lines)	Error: wrong orientation	Error: Wrong location	Error: Missing holes
LS	2%	35%	6%	17%	23%
MS	21%	27%	10%	11%	10%
HS	23%	47%	2%	11%	9%

Task 3 (Straight and Diagonal; Table 5). There was no significant difference in the association between spatial group and success for Task 3 (according to Chi-square statistics), $\chi^2(2, N = 147) = 5.53, p = .06$.

Table 5. Task 3 dominant responses (percentages based on spatial group).

Spatial Group	Correct (with lines)	Correct (no lines)	Error: Symmetrical arrangement	Error: Missing holes
LS	10%	33%	13%	36%
MS	9%	28%	24%	26%
HS	18%	43%	20%	15%

For LS students the most frequent errors occurred when too few holes were represented. As they rarely drew the lines for this item, we can only infer that students were not visualizing sufficient folds to correctly complete the task. For MS students, the most common error was also too few holes, followed by too many holes which resulted in a symmetrical arrangement.

Reported data indicated that success on the open-ended tasks came from an ability to retain multiple spatial images 'in the mind's eye' and/or the use of a visual tool (i.e., line-drawing heuristic) to support the management of multiple spatial displays. Subsequent analysis was undertaken to explore whether mathematics knowledge was related to success, especially in relation to the specific maneuvering of spatial information.

3.3   Paper Folding Links to Mathematics

Correlations were carried out to explore relations between the three mathematics content areas and performance on the PFT (see Table 6). For the PFT straight maneuver items the correlations were significant and relatively consistent across mathematics content areas. For the multidirectional items correlations were stronger for geometry-measurement content performance. This is understandable given the additional complexity of rotations and reflections based on diagonal folds.

Table 6. Correlations between the PFT and mathematics measures.

	PFT	PFT straight	PFT diagonal	PFT straight and diagonal
Number	$.375^{**}$	$.258^{**}$	$.115$	$.318^{**}$
Word	$.318^{**}$	$.258^{**}$	$.132$	$.291^{**}$
Geometry-Measurement	$.411^{**}$	$.289^{**}$	$.171^{*}$	$.423^{**}$

Note. $* p < .05$, $** p < .01$

Relationships between PFT diagonal tasks and mathematics understanding are weak. This suggests that any mechanisms that allow students to use logical reasoning or drawing heuristics are not being utilized. Rather, students rely on evoking visual representations alone to solve the tasks. This complements the findings reported in the previous section in which only the diagonal fold task success was associated with spatial skill.

Exploring Open-Ended Task Association with Mathematics. The association between performance on the mathematics test (broken down by content area) and the open-ended tasks based on spatial group are presented in Figs. 3, 4, and 5.

For Task 1 (Fig. 3), HS students who correctly solved the open-ended task consistently outperformed their HS peers across all mathematics content areas. By contrast, for MS students, this pattern was most noticeable for word problems and to a lesser extent GM tasks. Performance on word and GM problems was roughly equivalent for LS students, regardless of their success in solving the straight task.

There was variability in the association between success on Task 2 and mathematics was for HS students (Fig. 4). This is most evident for number items where the difference in performance was more than 1 (out of 6) and for GM, which was close to 2 (out of 10). There was a marginal advantage for successful LS students on word problems. Successful MS students approached a 1 item advantage on the GM measure but were

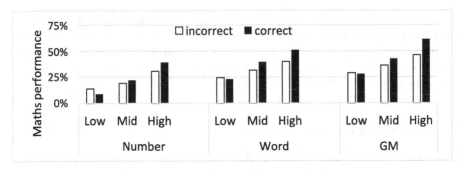

Fig. 3. Straight open-ended task success and links to mathematics.

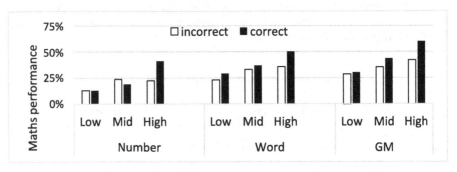

Fig. 4. Diagonal open-ended task success and links to mathematics.

only marginally better on the word problems. Performance on the number problems was low for LS and MS students, yet performance was too low to be meaningful.

Figure 5 reveals that the association between success on Task 3 and mathematics performance was evident for GM tasks for most students, and number tasks for HS students. The advantage for HS students in GM was marginal. There was no association between the multi-fold open-ended task and performance on the word problems.

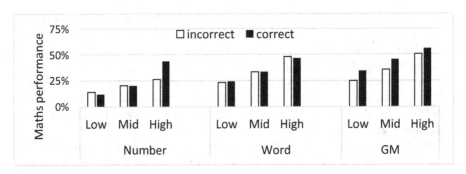

Fig. 5. Multi-fold (i.e., straight & diagonal) open-ended task success and links to mathematics.

4 Discussion

We explored the links between performance on the paper folding test (PFT), open-ended paper folding tasks and their association with mathematics. Performance on the PFT and its correlation with mathematics reinforces previous literature [1] and builds on existing work suggesting a distinction between the demands of straight and diagonal folds on paper folding measures [12, 20, 26]. Furthermore, the open-ended tasks demonstrated different levels of association across mathematics content and spatial skill level. Despite modest reliability, on average Grade 8 students were able to complete the PFT at a success rate over 50%. However, when the PFT items were broken down by the type of folds this was only true of the items with either straight or diagonal folds. Ramful [20] proposed that the diagonal fold was a source of difficulty for school-aged students, but here the combined effect of different fold directions was the most challenging. The difference in association between the types of folds and mathematics content indicates there may be various mechanisms for the different folding maneuvers within a single test, and therefore different affordances for mathematics [9, 12, 14].

When students were given an open-ended opportunity to complete paper folding tasks the success rates were highest among HS students overall. However, as the task was open-ended there was no chance option, yet LS and MS students still completed the task with reasonable success ranging from 30% to 47% of those who attempted the task. In fact, LS students who attempted Task 3 (with both straight and diagonal folds) had a higher success rate than their MS peers with response rates roughly equal to those in the HS category. Although the time factor is important from a spatial measurement perspective, these results indicate LS students may have efficient, albeit perhaps non-spatial, strategies for completing SV tasks [21].

4.1 Types of Folds and Use of Encoding Strategies

Based on the use of lines in the drawings, it seems that HS students were using more mental strategies (whether visualization or analytical is unclear) as nearly half the HS students represented the unfolded paper correctly without drawing the fold lines. Encoding strategies (such as the use of lines) are less helpful to HS students because they can readily store the visual processes in their minds' eye [14].

For the tasks that contained diagonal folds (2 and 3), more students were successful when they did not draw the fold lines. This contrasts with findings from Task 1 (straight) where LS and HS students were more often correct with the use of lines. A considerable proportion of the lines drawn incorrectly reflected the fold sequence, suggesting that spatial errors were occurring for LS and MS students. Drawings are an important representational scaffold as they allow students to store visual information more easily [14, 28]. However, without the requisite skills, students can end up encoding erroneous information into their representations [17].

The highest proportion of correct responses for the diagonal-only task was for HS students (70%), with roughly half MS students and just over a third of the LS students accurately representing the unfolded paper. This suggests there is an increased difficulty for the diagonal, compared with straight folds, however many HS students possessed strategies that ease this difficulty. The items that included straight folds did not have the same advantage for HS students, suggesting they may be employing a different set of strategies for the diagonal folds [20]. It is possible that students draw on logical reasoning for straight folds in a way that they can't for diagonal folds which require more spatial processing, hence the advantage for HS students.

In Task 3, the most frequent errors for LS and MS students involved missing holes where they effectively ignored the diagonal fold step or didn't see the relevance to the final arrangement. Students were able to complete the symmetrical object-to-object mapping typical of spatial visualization tasks in their representations [6], however sometimes this was to the point that they ignored steps in the folding sequence.

4.2 Spatial Relations and Structure

Spatial visualization tasks involve changes to the spatial relations within an object as well as structural changes to its form [5–7]. This study provides some evidence for the dissociation of these two aspects of the tasks. For example, the reflection over the fold lines is primarily about spatial relations while the resulting arrays in the holes are about structure. Both relate to the nature of the folds but some of the items in both the open-ended tasks and the PFT disrupted students' ideas of reflection and arrays.

In Task 2, errors were related to both structure and spatial relations. Many students placed the rotated array in the wrong location on the page, despite the folded shape and holes being in the bottom of the folded page. Students tended to move the arrangement to the top of the page when they imagined it unfolding. Alternatively, errors were found in the orientation of the holes, as students tended to represent prototypical 2×2 arrays, despite the series of folds being diagonal [26].

Symmetry is a central idea in mathematics [19] and therefore it makes sense that students would seek to recreate this symmetry in the open-ended task. However, there are rules that exist with reflections across axes that may be difficult to visualize. For example, on reflection, a diagonal line changes the orientation of the resulting arrangement. Thus, if an object is oriented diagonally to the left it will be oriented to the right on reflection [20]. Task 2 was a series of diagonal folds that had a very high success rate amongst HS students suggesting some awareness of this spatial relation [6].

4.3 Spatial Associations with Mathematics

It was evident across most mathematics content that HS students were able to employ similar successful (spatial) strategies for the open-ended tasks as they did for the mathematics assessment. For the straight task, HS students who were able to encode successfully in the open-ended spatial task showed an advantage across the board in mathematics. For MS students, an advantage was evident for word problems and to a degree in GM. The straight fold task was not straight forward, it had a level of complexity and spatial sophistication not found in the PFT straight items. Students needed to extract the relevant information from the sequence of pictures and encode these steps in their representation. The same applies when solving word problems [14, 17, 22]. The absence of any association between the straight fold task and performance in mathematics for LS students may suggest that these students are using different strategies [29].

The only noteworthy variability on the diagonal task was for HS students, therefore when they were more accurate on the diagonal spatial task (i.e., can perform the complex sequence of spatial maneuvers in their minds correctly) they are also performing better on the mathematics tasks across the board. The open-ended tasks that included straight folds (Tasks 1 and 3) had more logical components to decipher, whereas students may not possess intuitive strategies to utilize any logical structures to help solve diagonal tasks. Even though visualization is important in novel situations [30] when tasks become complex, the mental load can be too much for some students without logical reasoning or effective use of spatial tools [12, 14].

HS students were completing close to 50% of the GM and word items correctly regardless of their performance on Task 3 (straight and diagonal fold). MS students who correctly solved Task 3 had similar performance levels as HS students in GM, their toolkit of spatial strategies may have helped in both situations [14]. Task 3 revealed an association with the GM tasks for LS students (i.e., those that integrated spatial and analytical elements will do better in geometry).

There was an association with number tasks for HS students. It is likely that strong spatial skills support students to perform complex mental maneuvers as well as mental calculations [2, 14]. The volume and multiple directions of the folds in Task 3 meant that many students were not able to attend to changes in both structure and relations, with many opting to focus on the spatial relations between the holes at the expense of the broader structural relations associated with the folds. This was evident in the pattern of errors, which were dominated by the production of symmetrical arrays. Further evidence is in the lack of association with success on word problems for all students as the SV skill underpinning performance on word problems is the ability to encode structural relations [14].

4.4 Limitations

This study emerged from a larger project [22] and therefore, the analysis was driven by the data available to address our research question [31] resulting in some unavoidable limitations. For example, using the PFT to categorize students based on spatial skill and then analyzing performance on an analogous task is somewhat circular. Future work could use categorization based on dissociated or composite measures.

The low reliability of the PFT has also been reported in previous studies [20, 22]. It is possible this relates to the different demands of the various folds within the test. Future work may examine both parts of the test with a greater number of items enabling the exploration of the psychometrics of these subscales separately.

The post-hoc nature of analysis of the collected workbook data resulted in primarily descriptive analysis. The results stimulated ideas for future research that may build on theories about the mechanistic link between paper folding and mathematics. For example, the evidence that students were using different processes for diagonal compared with straight folds could be unpacked further with more items and think-aloud protocols to explore the cognitive processes at an in-depth level.

Instances of students missing holes or lines are indicative of skipped steps in the sequence and may suggest difficulties with spatial working memory (WM) capacity which was not measured in the present study. Future work could examine the role WM plays and whether scaffolded instructions for offloading some of the mental load through drawings could transfer to students' mathematical problem-solving [14].

4.5 Implications and Future Directions

Mix [14] debated whether the functional role of spatial reasoning in mathematics is due to the automatic recruitment of spatial processes or intentional, strategic use of spatial representations. The results of this study indicate that it may depend on spatial skills and strategies. Some HS students implicitly used similar strategies for spatial and mathematics tasks while some MS students made intentional use of spatial representations. The key to success was the complementary use of visualization skills and spatial tools to map appropriate spatial representations. From this we infer that development of both isolated spatial skills (through training), and flexible use of spatial tools (through pedagogy) are necessary to support mathematics problem-solving [9, 12].

Although LS students struggled with the PFT, many were successful on the untimed, open-ended tasks, albeit with no association with their mathematics performance. It is possible they employed different strategies on the open-ended tasks to offset their spatial skills [29] or with sufficient time outside of the testing environment, they can apply analytic strategies that help them solve spatial tasks [21, 32]. Unpacking this trend is important to support LS students in mathematics. Studies have shown that if students receive explicit training in making connections between spatial skills and logical reasoning patterns, performance on both spatial and mathematics tasks improve [12].

Acknowledgments. This study was funded by the Australian Research Council (DP150101961).

Disclosure of Interests.   The authors have no competing interests to declare that are relevant to the content of this article.

References

1. Xie, F., Zhang, L., Chen, X., Xin, Z.: Is spatial ability related to mathematical ability: a meta-analysis. Educ. Psychol. Rev. **32**(1), 113–155 (2020)
2. Hawes, Z., Gilligan-Lee, K.A., Mix, K.S.: Effects of spatial training on mathematics performance: a meta-analysis. Dev. Psychol. **58**(1), 112–137 (2022)
3. Ramful, A., Ho, S.Y., Lowrie, T.: Visual and analytical strategies in spatial visualisation: perspectives from bilateral symmetry and reflection. Math. Educ. Res.h J. **27**(4), 443–470 (2015)
4. Ramful, A., Lowrie, T., Logan, T.: Measurement of spatial ability: construction and validation of the spatial reasoning instrument for middle school students. J. Psychoeduc. Assess. **35**(7), 709–727 (2017)
5. Höffler, T.N.: Spatial ability: Its influence on learning with visualizations – a meta-analytic review. Educ. Psychol. Rev. **22**(3), 245–269 (2010)
6. Kozhevnikov, M., Hegarty, M.: A dissociation between object manipulation spatial ability and spatial orientation ability. Mem. Cognit. **29**(5), 745–756 (2001)

7. Sezen Yüksel, N.: Measuring spatial visualization: test development study. In: Khine, M. (eds.) Visual-spatial ability in STEM education. Springer, Cham (2017). https://doi.org/10.1007/978-3-319-44385-0_4

8. Ekstrom, R.B., French, J.W., Harman, H.H., Dermen, D.: Kit of factor-referenced cognitive tests. Educ. Test. Serv. (1976)

9. Hawes, Z., Gilligan-Lee, K.A., Mix, K.S.: Infusing spatial thinking into middle school mathematics: what, why, and how? In: Robinson, K.M., Dubé, A., Kostopoulos, D. (eds.), Mathematical cognition and understanding, pp. 13–33 (2023). Springer, Cham. https://doi.org/10.1007/978-3-031-29195-1_2

10. Gilligan, K.A., Thomas, M.S., Farran, E.K.: First demonstration of effective spatial training for near transfer to spatial performance and far transfer to a range of mathematics skills at 8 years. Develop. Sci. **23**(4) (2020)

11. Harris, D.: Spatial reasoning in context: Bridging cognitive and educational perspectives of spatial-mathematics relations. Front. Educ. **8** (2023)

12. Lowrie, T., Logan, T.: Spatial visualization supports students' math: mechanisms for spatial transfer. J. Intell. **11**(6), 127 (2023)

13. Lowrie, T., Resnick, I., Harris, D., Logan, T.: In search of the mechanisms that enable transfer from spatial reasoning to mathematics understanding. Math. Educ. Res. J. **32**(2), 175–188 (2020)

14. Mix, K.S.: Why are spatial skill and mathematics related? Child Develop. Perspect. **13**(2), 121–126 (2019)

15. Yu, M., Cui, J., Wang, L., Gao, X., Cui, Z., Zhou, X.: Spatial processing rather than logical reasoning was found to be critical for mathematical problem-solving. Learn. Individ. Differ. **100**, 102230 (2022)

16. Battista, M.T., Frazee, L.M., Winer, M.L.: Analyzing the relation between spatial and geometric reasoning for elementary and middle school students. In: Mix, K., Battista, M. (eds.) Visualizing mathematics. Research in Mathematics Education. Springer, Cham (2018). https://doi.org/10.1007/978-3-319-98767-5_10

17. Hegarty, M., Kozhevnikov, M.: Types of visual-spatial representations and mathematical problem solving. J. Educ. Psychol. **91**(4), 684–689 (1999)

18. Empson, S.B., Turner, E.: The emergence of multiplicative thinking in children's solutions to paper folding tasks. J. Math. Behav. **25**(1), 46–56 (2006)

19. Ng, O., Sinclair, N.: Young children reasoning about symmetry in a dynamic geometry environment. ZDM **47**, 421–434 (2015)

20. Ramful, A.: Psychometric properties of the paper folding test. [Conference session]. SERC Spatial Reasoning Conference, Canberra, Australia (2018)

21. Uttal, D.H., McKee, K., Simms, N., Hegarty, M., Newcombe, N.S.: How can we best assess spatial skills? Practical and conceptual challenges. J. Intell. **12** (2024)

22. Lowrie, T., Harris, D., Logan, T., Hegarty, M.: The impact of a spatial intervention program on students' spatial reasoning and mathematics performance. J. Exper. Educ. **89**(2), 259–277 (2021)

23. Lohman, D.F.: Cognitive Abilities Test, Form 7, book 11: Paper Folding. Houghton Mifflin Harcourt (2012)

24. Blazhenkova, O., Becker, M., Kozhevnikov, M.: Object-spatial imagery and verbal cognitive styles in children and adolescents: developmental trajectories in relation to ability. Learn. Individ. Differ. **21**(3), 281–287 (2011)

25. Boonen, A.J.H., van Wesel, F., Jolles, J., van der Schoot, M.: The role of visual representation type, spatial ability, and reading comprehension in word problem solving: an item-level analysis in elementary school children. Int. J. Educ. Res. **68**, 15–26 (2014)

26. Ho, S.Y., Logan, T.: Students' performance on a symmetry task. In: Steinle, V., Ball, L., Bardini, C. (eds.), Mathematics Education: Yesterday, today and tomorrow (Proceedings of the 36th annual conference of the Mathematics Education Research Group of Australasia), pp. 747–750. MERGA, Melbourne, Australia (2013)
27. Australian F-10 Curriculum: Mathematics. http://www.australiancurriculum.edu.au/mathematics/curriculum/f-10?layout=1. Accessed 23 Jan 2024
28. Logan, T., Lowrie, T., Diezmann, C.M.: Co-thought gestures: supporting students to successfully navigate map tasks. Educ. Stud. Math. **87**(1), 87–102 (2014)
29. Harris, D., Logan, T., Lowrie, T.: Spatial visualization and measurement of area: A case study in spatialized mathematics instruction. J. Math. Behav. **70** (2023)
30. Uttal, D.H., Cohen, C.A.: Spatial thinking and STEM education: when, why, and how? In: Ross, B. (ed.), Psychology of learning and motivation, vol. 57. Academic Press (2012)
31. Logan, T.: Sustaining mathematics education research: a secondary data analysis framework [Unpublished doctoral dissertation]. University of Canberra (2019)
32. Nolte, N., Schmitz, F., Fleischer, J., Bungart, M., Leutner, D.: Rotational complexity in mental rotation tests: cognitive processes in tasks requiring mental rotation around cardinal and skewed rotation axes. Intelligence **91**, 101626 (2022)

Mindset Matters: The Role of Mathematics Self-concept and Age in Mental Rotation Performance Among Primary School Children

Michelle Lennon-Maslin$^{(\boxtimes)}$ and Claudia Quaiser-Pohl

Faculty of Educational Sciences, Department of Developmental Psychology and Psychological Assessment, Institute of Psychology, University of Koblenz, Koblenz, Germany
mlennonm@uni-koblenz.de

Abstract. This cross-sectional study investigates the role of maths self-concept in spatial skills development among primary school children. The study, conducted on a sample of students (mean age $M = 8.48$, $SD = 1.11$) consisting of 70 girls and 74 boys, explores the relationship between maths self-concept and mental rotation skills, with a focus on gender and the stage of childhood development. Students completed a computerized mental rotation task measuring accuracy and response time and a maths self-concept questionnaire. Results reveal girls and tweens (pre-adolescents) demonstrate lower maths self-concept compared to boys and younger children. Moreover, maths self-concept and the stage of childhood development significantly influence mental rotation performance, with those with higher self-concept and tweens scoring better on the task. These findings emphasize the importance of addressing low maths self-concept, particularly in girls and students transitioning to secondary education, to foster spatial skills development. Targeted support during this critical educational phase is crucial.

Keywords: Mathematics Self-Concept · Stage of Childhood Development · Mental Rotation Skills

1 Introduction

"I must tell you what my opinion of my own mind and powers is exactly … I believe myself to possess a most singular combination of qualities exactly fitted to make me pre-eminently a discoverer of the hidden realities of nature"
−Ada Noel King, *The Bride Of Science* [1]

This cross-sectional study focuses on the role of maths self-concept and spatial ability in a sample of primary school children at two different stages of childhood development.

This article is written in British English.

M. Živković et al. (Eds.): Spatial Cognition 2024, LNAI 14756, pp. 19–31, 2024.
https://doi.org/10.1007/978-3-031-63115-3_2

1.1 Mathematical Skills: Nature or Nurture?

Mathematics or maths, often overshadowed in STEM discussions, serves as the foundational language of science, technology, and engineering [2]. Recent studies reveal individual differences in brain and genetic predisposition for maths [3]. However, a biopsychosocial perspective underscores the role of environment, attitudes, emotions, as well as biology in mathematical skills development. Contrary to fixed abilities, research supports the malleability of maths skills, even in low-performing students [4]. Expertise in maths is attributed to extended and intense training [5]. Understanding and addressing attitudes toward maths are crucial for removing obstacles and improving student outcomes in performance.

1.2 Maths Self-concept and Its Impact on Maths Achievement

There is evidence that humans are born sensitive to numeracy and that in fact, attitudes and perceptions as well as classroom experience shape children's beliefs about their mathematical ability [6]. Many people attribute an anxiety or dislike of maths to negative experiences during their school years leading to decreased engagement with the subject [7]. Maths frequently serves as that academic domain in which children encounter significant challenges, characterized by profound setbacks, a circumstance further compounded by the responses of educators and attitudes adopted by parents [8, 9]. These experiences shape what is referred to as maths self-concept, or how children think about themselves in relation to maths. It is known to impact children's engagement with the subject because it pertains to how confident an individual feels about their ability to learn new mathematical topics, perform well in class, and do well on maths tests [10, 11]. Moreover, the Reciprocal Effects Model (REM) posits a mutually reinforcing relationship between self-concept and academic achievement over time. According to this theoretical framework, proficiency in mathematics fosters a positive self-concept in students, which, in turn, contributes to enhanced performance [12]. Encouraging active involvement and participation in mathematics is therefore anticipated to yield positive effects on students' self-concept. Studies conducted in the United States and China with pre- and primary school children found a reciprocal relationship between maths self-concept, interest, and achievement [13, 14]. In essence, maths self-concept is an important factor accounting for differences in school children's mathematical achievement with the socialisation process having a significant effect.

1.3 Mental Rotation and Its Relationship with Mathematics Skills

Extensively studied in psychology and education, mental rotation (MR), the ability to mentally rotate two- and three-dimensional objects, is a key aspect of spatial ability in which significant gender differences have been noted [15]. The established connection between spatial and mathematical ability is reinforced by a recent meta-analysis, suggesting that spatial training enhances comprehension and performance in mathematics [16]. MR, a predictor of mathematical ability in pre- and primary school children, is also linked to academic success and career choices in STEM fields [17]. Similar to maths skills, MR ability can be enhanced through practice and training [18].

1.4 Gender Differences in Maths Self-concept and the Impact on STEM as a Career Choice

While Ada Lovelace displayed confidence in her intellectual abilities, many present-day girls and women appear less assured in their mathematical skills. Despite their advancements in STEM, women's under-representation in maths-intensive university programs such as engineering, computer science, and physics may be attributed to insufficient maths self-concept [19]. Research with adults indicates that, despite similar maths achievement, women exhibit lower self-concept than men [20]. Initially, girls may perform equally well or even surpass boys in maths achievement, but a shift occurs as they progress through the education system, particularly in the upper skill levels [21]. The gender gap in higher maths achievement is concerning, as it negatively affects the pipeline for future STEM professionals [22].

1.5 Stereotype Threat and Its Impact on How Children and Young People Relate to Maths and STEM

Stereotype threat (ST) refers to situations in which individuals feel at risk of confirming negative stereotypes about their in-group [23]. Common stereotypes associated with excellence in maths and other STEM fields include the "nerd" or "geek". This concept portrays individuals as male, disproportionately intelligent but socially awkward and romantically unsuccessful [24, 25]. Such stereotypes adversely impact the appeal of STEM subjects such as maths, especially for girls and young people.

The tween or pre-adolescent stage (approx. 9 to 12 years old) is a crucial period for identity exploration, where self-concept and stereotypes become more prominent. Tweens undergo neurodevelopmental changes, heightened executive functioning, and increased awareness of gender identity and societal hierarchies and norms [26]. This stage precedes a significant educational transition, with tweens making important decisions about their secondary education focus. While becoming aware of negative stereotypes, tweens are sensitive to societal expectations, influencing their choices and engagement with subjects like maths [27].

Research confirms the endorsement of the "STEM-nerd" stereotype among secondary school students in the USA and middle-school students in Germany [24, 28]. This stereotype undermines interest in STEM fields due to a fear of conforming to negative expectations, particularly for females who are often expected to strive for attractiveness, sociability, and romantic success [29].

1.6 Rationale and Aims of the Current Study

This study addresses key factors related to primary school children's maths self-concept and spatial ability development. Despite being perceived as challenging, maths can be a rewarding subject for children, with its achievement linked to improved socio-economic prospects and opportunities for those who wish to pursue a career in STEM fields [30]. Girls' maths self-concept is crucial for their progression in STEM, and may help surpass the "leaky pipeline" phenomenon where female students abandon STEM aspirations at various education stages [31]. Importantly, maths self-concept is malleable, offering intervention opportunities for improved outcomes for all children.

Proficiency in spatial abilities has been shown to correlate with motivational factors such as mathematics self-efficacy and maths anxiety among youth [32]. Therefore, the study explores the role of maths self-concept in MR performance, measured by accuracy and response time on the task, in primary school children. It aims to understand whether maths self-concept contributes to differences, including gender disparities, in MR performance, providing insights for enhancing maths and STEM engagement and reducing gender gaps in STEM fields.

1.7 Hypotheses

As children progress through primary school, societal and peer influences become more pronounced, potentially impacting their self-concept in maths. In girls, the stereotype that associates maths with male dominance and intellectual competence can reinforce stereotype threat with a risk of negatively affecting performance [33].

During the tween years, children may become more aware of negative societal stereotypes related to maths and STEM, leading them to avoid confirming these. Additionally, the increasing academic demands and complexity of maths concepts in late primary education may contribute to decreased self-concept if children struggle to meet these expectations [34]. On the other hand, younger children in middle childhood may have a more positive and uninhibited view of their abilities, leading to higher maths self-concept scores compared to their older counterparts [35].

Hypothesis 1.: *We expect that there will be significant gender and age differences in maths self-concept in primary school students. Specifically, girls will have sinifcantly lower maths self-concept than boys. Tweens (9-to-11-year-olds) will have significantly lower maths self-concept than students in middle childhood (6-to-8-year-olds).*

Gender differences in MR skills have been extensively studied due to a persistent disparity in the ability of males and females found in this domain [36, 37]. The gender gap has also been established amongst children, with boys demonstrating better scores and faster speed of processing on tests of MR [38]. Maths self-concept has been identified as an important motivational factor accounting for enhanced performance on mathematical and spatial tasks [32].

As neurodevelopment advances, notably in the prefrontal and parietal cortex (brain regions associated with spatial skills development), children typically experience improvements in cognitive abilities, including spatial reasoning skills [39]. Furthermore, children in late primary education are likely to have had greater exposure to spatial tasks and activities, both within and outside of educational settings, compared to younger children [40].

Hypothesis 2.: *We expect there will be significant individual differences in accuracy and response time on a MR task. Moreover, these differences depend on a student's gender, stage of childhood development and maths self-concept. Tweens will be more accurate and have shorter response times than students in middle childhood. Students with high maths self-concept will be more accurate and have shorter response times than students with low maths self-concept.*

2 Materials and Methods

2.1 Participants

One hundred and forty-four students were recruited from primary schools in the state of Rhineland Palatinate, Germany ($N = 144$). All of the students were enrolled in local primary schools. Seventy-four students identified as boys ($N = 74$, *Mean age* = 8.55 years) and seventy as girls ($N = 70$, *Mean age* = 8.47 years). The average age of all students was $M = 8.47$ ($SD = 1.23$) years old. The distribution of students by age is shown in Table 1.

Table 1. Age Distribution of Participating Students

		Frequency	Percent
Valid	6	6	4.2
	7	21	14.6
	8	45	31.3
	9	46	31.9
	10	23	16.0
	11	3	2.1
	Total	144	100.0

2.2 Material and Instrumentation

Mental Rotation Task

A computerized Mental Rotation task (MRT) was developed using PsychoPy® software on Microsoft Pro 8 Surface tablets with a keyboard and mouse. The task assessed accuracy and response time, featuring MR stimuli for younger children such as animals, letters, and cubes [41], as well as abstract and concrete stimuli rotated in picture-plane and in-depth. Abstract items included cubes, pellets [15, 42], and polyhedral figures [43]. Concrete items comprised gender-stereotyped stimuli: male, female, and neutral objects [44]. The task had two parts with time limits: Part one (MRT 1) had 16 items (6 abstract, 10 concrete) rotated in picture plane within a 5-min limit. Part two (MRT 2) included 12 items (6 abstract, 6 concrete) with stimuli rotated in-depth, allowed 8 min. Items were presented randomly with one target on the left and four comparisons on the right, and participants identified identical rotated stimuli. A reliability analysis of the task based on our sample data yielded a Cronbach's Alpha of $\alpha = .86$.

Demographic Data and Questionnaires

An online questionnaire was presented to each participant to collect data relating to their age and gender. A self-report questionnaire was also created in PsychoPy® and, to avoid priming, was presented following the MRT.

Maths Self-concept in Primary School Children

Students completed the Maths Self-Concept Subscale of the Academic Self-Concept Questionnaire for Primary School Children (ASKG) [45]. This is a German self-report measure based on Marsh, Byrne, and Shavelson's (1988) revised hierarchical self-concept model [46]. The subscale has 6 items and assesses maths self-concept on a 7-point sliding scale. Items prompt participants to rate their ability and enjoyment of mathematics. A reliability analysis of the mathematics self-concept subscale conducted on our sample data yielded a Cronbach's Alpha of $\alpha = .90$.

2.3 Procedure

Approval for the pilot study was granted by the Ethics Committee of the University of Koblenz and the relevant state authorities overseeing schools in Rhineland Palatine. Informed consent from parents and guardians, as well as permission from the class teacher and principal, was obtained. Students provided verbal assent, were informed about their right to withdraw at any point without consequences, and were tested by two female researchers in a well-lit, separate classroom with individual seating. The MRT was explained through physical object rotations, emphasizing the importance of MR in daily life and school work.

3   Results

3.1   Differences in Mathematics Self-Concept Based on Gender and Age in Primary School Children

An independent samples t-test revealed a significant difference in maths self-concept between males ($M = 28.85$, $SD = 7.06$) and females ($M = 25.57$, $SD = 7.67$), $t(141) = 2.67$, $p = .009$, CI (95%) $0.850 -> 5.72$ with a small to medium effect size ($d = .45$), indicating that girls exhibited significantly lower maths self-concept than boys.

Similarly, a second independent samples t-test showed a significant difference in maths self-concept between the middle childhood group ($M = 28.67$, $SD = 7.24$) and the tween group ($M = 25.69$, $SD = 7.65$), $t(142) = 2.41$, $p = .017$, CI (95%) $0.54 ->$ 5.42, with a small to medium effect size ($d = .40$), with the tween group demonstrating significantly lower maths self-concept than the middle childhood group.

3.2   Differences in Accuracy and Response Time on the MRT Based on Gender, Stage of Childhood Development, and Maths Self-Concept

A two-way multivariate analysis of variance (MANOVA) was conducted, with the composite dependent variable combining Accuracy and Response Time on the MRT. The independent variables examined were Gender, Stage of Childhood Development and Maths Self-Concept. The results indicate there was no main effect of Gender (F (1, 143) $= 1.85$, $p = .162$; $\eta p 2 = .03$) in accuracy and response time in the MRT. However, there was a significant main effect Stage of Childhood Development (F (1, 143) $= 4.95$, $p = .008$; $\eta p 2 = .07$) and of Maths Self-Concept (F (1, 143) $= 3.16$, $p = .046$; $\eta p 2 = .05$) (see Table 2).

Table 2. Multivariate Tests: Main Effects of Stage of Childhood Development (Dev_Stage) and Maths Self-Concept (MSC) on Accuracy and Response Time on the Mental Rotation Task.

Effect	Value		F	Hypothesis df	Error df	Sig	Partial Eta Squared
Dev_Stage	Wilks Lambda	.069	4.947	2.000	134.000	.008	.069
MSC	Wilks Lambda	.045	3.162	2.000	134.000	.046	.045

a. Design: Intercept + Sex + Dev_Stage + MSC + Sex * Dev_Stage + Sex * MSC + Dev_Stage * MSC + Sex * Dev_Stage * MSC

Following a Bonferroni adjustment at .025, there was a significant effect of Stage of Childhood Development (F (1, 143) = 9.96, p = .002) with a medium to large effect size ($\eta p 2$ = .07) suggesting that Stage of Childhood Development explains a substantial portion of the variance in accuracy on the MRT. Furthermore, there was a significant main effect of Maths Self-Concept (F (1, 143) = 6.26, p = .014) with a small effect size ($\eta p 2$ = .04) indicating that Maths Self-Concept accounts for a meaningful proportion of the variance in accuracy on the MRT.

Pairwise comparisons highlighted tweens scored higher than students in middle childhood (*Mean Difference* = .09, p = .002, 95% (*CI*) .04 - .16) on the MRT (s. Table 3). Additionally, students with higher Maths Self-Concept scored higher than those with lower Maths Self-Concept (*Mean Difference* = .08, p = .014, 95% (*CI*) .02 - .14) (s. Fig. 1).

There was no effect of Gender, Stage of Childhood Development or Maths Self-Concept on response times on the MRT (F (1, 143) = .06, p = .805, $\eta p 2$ = .00).

Table 3. Pairwise Comparisons: Tweens Scored Higher than Students in Middle Childhood on the Mental Rotation Task.

Dependent Variable	(I) DevStage	(J) DevStage	Mean Difference (I-J)	Std. Error	Sig.[b]	95% Confidence Interval for Difference[b]	
						Lower Bound	Upper Bound
Accuracy on the MRT	Tweens	Middle Childhood	.099*	.031	.002	.037	.161

Based on estimated marginal means
*. The mean difference is significant at the .05 level
b. Adjustment for multiple comparisons: Bonferroni

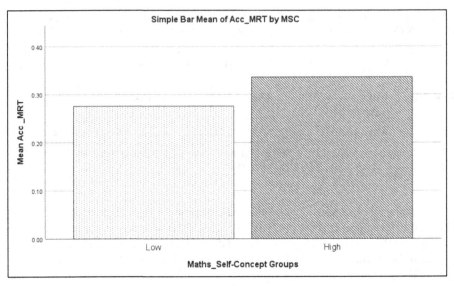

Fig. 1. Effects of Maths Self-Concept (MSC) on Students' Accuracy in the Mental Rotation Task (Acc_MRT).

4   Discussion

4.1   Unlocking Potential: Gender and Age Differences in Maths Self-Concept in Primary Education

In this study, primary school girls and students in the tween stage exhibited lower maths self-concept compared to boys and middle childhood peers. Considering the relationship between maths self-concept and maths achievement, this finding suggests that gender and age differences in maths performance may be attributable to girls' and tweens' lack of identification with maths as a school subject. This finding may be based on students' misconceptions and stereotyped beliefs about STEM fields being only for the mathematically gifted. Early interventions, such as peer mentoring for girls and children in the tween stage, may counteract negative attitudes and maintain engagement with maths going forward. The study highlights the importance of addressing low maths self-concept early in education to prevent potential disengagement from STEM subjects going forward. Interventions such as peer mentoring for girls and tweens have already revealed favorable results in Europe and the United States [47, 48].

4.2   Tween Challenge: Differences in Mental Rotation Performance Based on Stage of Childhood Development

In our study, the stage of childhood development emerged as the most influential factor to play a role in students' performance on the MRT. Despite tweens exhibiting lower levels of maths self-concept, they demonstrated significantly higher accuracy on the task. This incongruity suggests a combination of neurodevelopmental growth and the impact of education have a positive effect on spatial skill development. However, low levels of maths self-concept have previously been identified amongst students in the upper tiers of the mathematical skills distribution, an issue that could hinder achievement and progression in STEM in further education. Therefore, our findings underscore the critical importance of addressing low maths self-concept in the tween age group to prevent disengagement from maths and related subjects. Fortunately, the malleability of maths self-concept indicates that targeted interventions during this sensitive stage have the potential to attract more young people to STEM fields, broadening their future options.

4.3 Counteracting Stereotypes: Differences in Mental Rotation Performance Based on Gender and Maths Self-Concept

Contrary to much of the research on the subject of MR, we found no significant differences in accuracy and response times on the MRT based on gender. Our MRT included stimuli with male, female, and neutral objects as well as abstract objects known to be gender-neutral which may have reduced the power of stereotypes [43, 49].

We found no differences in response times on the MRT based on gender, age, or maths self-concept. Time limits on our task were longer than on classic tests of MR to allow for individual differences in processing strategies [50]. Therefore, while certain factors such as maths self-concept and stage of childhood development play a role in students' precision on spatial tasks, they do not necessarily impact their efficiency or speed of processing. Future research might explore other underlying mechanisms affecting the cognitive processing of spatial tasks such as emotional reactivity. Maths and spatial anxiety, for example, are known to have differentiated effects on girls' and boys' performance on spatial tasks [51, 52].

In our study, a significant link was found between maths self-concept and performance on the MRT. Students with low maths self-concept exhibited significantly lower accuracy on the MRT compared to those with high maths self-concept. This underscores the interconnectedness of attitudes towards mathematics and achievement in spatial tasks. The association between low engagement with maths and spatial activities suggests that children with low maths self-concept may lack the necessary practice and skills in order to accurately solve complex spatial tasks such as MR. This finding indicates that mathematically confident students are potentially more motivated to engage effectively in spatial tasks. Due to the small effect size found in the MANOVA, the findings warrant further investigation into other factors which play a role in counteracting students' stereotyped beliefs about maths and which boost performance on spatial tasks.

4.4 Limitations and Future Research

This study has certain limitations that should be considered. Firstly, it did not measure maths performance, which will be addressed in a future study to demonstrate how this relates to maths self-concept and MR skills. To enhance the study's findings, future research might also incorporate collection of maths and spatial anxiety as well as physiological data, providing complementary evidence. Moreover, the age distribution of the sample follows a bell curve with the youngest and oldest at the end of the distribution implying the results per age group analysis warrant further investigation. A longitudinal study for example, which follows a cohort of school children through their primary education, might demonstrate the development of maths self-concept and its relationship to maths achievement and MR performance over a longer period.

5   Conclusion

This study sheds light on crucial factors influencing children's performance in mathematics and spatial tasks in primary school. It underscores the importance of addressing low maths self-concept, particularly among girls and during the tween years. A key finding is the persistent gender and age disparities in maths self-concept highlighting enduring negative stereotypes that maths is a school subject preferred by boys and maths enthusiasts. The study provides evidence for the importance of early interventions to ensure academic choices are based on ability rather than attitudes. Moreover, evidence of the reinforcing relationship between maths self-concept and precision on MRTs, there is a clear need for tailored assessments and interventions to support spatial skills development in primary education. In summary, the study contributes to understanding of the interplay between self-concept and spatial ability in school children and underscores the importance of proactive interventions to empower them in embracing mathematics, STEM subjects, and spatial tasks, expanding their educational and career horizons.

Acknowledgments. Sincere thanks to the principals, teachers, parents and the students of the five schools who took part in our study. Without your participation, this research would not have been possible. This article is dedicated to the Ada Lovelace Project (ADL) who have been inspiring girls and young women in STEM for two and a half decades. I wish you, the ADL mentors, and their mentees many more successful years ahead.

Disclosure of Interests. The authors declare that the research was conducted in the absence of any commercial or financial relationships that could be construed as a potential conflict of interest.

References

1. Wooley, B.: Bride of science. London (2000)
2. Just, J., Siller, H.-S.: The role of mathematics in STEM secondary classrooms: a systematic literature review. Educ. Sci. **12**, 629 (2022). https://doi.org/10.3390/educsci12090629
3. Chen, H., et al.: A genome-wide association study identifies genetic variants associated with mathematics ability. Sci. Rep. **7**, 40365 (2017). https://doi.org/10.1038/srep40365
4. Lopez-Pedersen, A., Mononen, R., Aunio, P., Scherer, R., Melby-Lervåg, M.: Improving numeracy skills in first graders with low performance in early numeracy: a randomized controlled trial. Remed. Special Educ. **44**, 126–136 (2023). https://doi.org/10.1177/074193252 21102537
5. Sella, F., Cohen Kadosh, R.: What expertise can tell about mathematical learning and cognition. Mind Brain Educ. **12**, 186–192 (2018). https://doi.org/10.1111/mbe.12179
6. Attard, C.: "If I had to pick any subject, it wouldn't be maths": foundations for engagement with mathematics during the middle years. Math. Ed. Res. J. **25**, 569–587 (2013). https://doi.org/10.1007/s13394-013-0081-8

7. Boaler, J.: The elephant in the classroom: helping children learn and love maths. Souvenir Press (2015)
8. Davadas, S.D., Lay, Y.F.: Factors affecting students' attitude toward mathematics: a structural equation modeling approach. EURASIA J Math. Sci. Tech. Ed. **14**, 517–529 (2017). https://doi.org/10.12973/ejmste/80356
9. Rossnan, S.: Overcoming math anxiety. Mathitudes **1**, 4 (2006)
10. Bringula, R., Reguyal, J.J., Tan, D.D., Ulfa, S.: Mathematics self-concept and challenges of learners in an online learning environment during COVID-19 pandemic. Smart Learn. Environ. **8**, 22 (2021). https://doi.org/10.1186/s40561-021-00168-5
11. Cvencek, D., Paz-Albo, J., Master, A., Herranz Llácer, C.V., Hervás-Escobar, A., Meltzoff, A.N.: Math is for me: a field intervention to strengthen math self-concepts in Spanish-speaking 3rd grade children. Front. Psychol. **11**, 593995 (2020). https://doi.org/10.3389/fpsyg.2020.593995
12. Marsh, H.W., Craven, R.G.: Reciprocal effects of self-concept and performance from a multidimensional perspective: beyond seductive pleasure and unidimensional perspectives. Perspect. Psychol. Sci. **1**, 133–163 (2006). https://doi.org/10.1111/j.1745-6916.2006.00010.x
13. Cai, D., Viljaranta, J., Georgiou, G.K.: Direct and indirect effects of self-concept of ability on math skills. Learn. Individ. Differ. **61**, 51–58 (2018). https://doi.org/10.1016/j.lindif.2017.11.009
14. Fisher, P.H., Dobbs-Oates, J., Doctoroff, G.L., Arnold, D.H.: Early math interest and the development of math skills. J. Educ. Psychol. **104**, 673–681 (2012). https://doi.org/10.1037/a0027756
15. Neuburger, S., Ruthsatz, V., Jansen, P., Quaiser-Pohl, C.: Can girls think spatially? Influence of implicit gender stereotype activation and rotational axis on fourth graders' mental-rotation performance. Learn. Individ. Differ. **37**, 169–175 (2015). https://doi.org/10.1016/j.lindif.2014.09.003
16. Hawes, Z., Moss, J., Caswell, B., Poliszczuk, D.: Effects of mental rotation training on children's spatial and mathematics performance: a randomized controlled study. Trends Neurosci. Educ. **3**, 60–68 (2015). https://doi.org/10.1016/j.tine.2015.05.001
17. Moe, A.: Mental rotation and mathematics: gender-stereotyped beliefs and relationships in primary school children. Learn. Individ. Diff.. **61**, 172–180 (2018). https://doi.org/10.1016/j.lindif.2017.12.002
18. Uttal, D.H., et al.: The malleability of spatial skills: a meta-analysis of training studies. Psychol. Bull. **139**, 352–402 (2013). https://doi.org/10.1037/a0028446
19. Ceci, S.J., Ginther, D.K., Kahn, S., Williams, W.M.: Women in academic science: a changing landscape. Psychol. Sci. Public Interest **15**, 75–141 (2014). https://doi.org/10.1177/1529100614541236
20. Sax, L.J., Kanny, M.A., Riggers-Piehl, T.A., Whang, H., Paulson, L.N.: "But I'm Not Good at Math": the changing salience of mathematical self-concept in shaping women's and men's STEM aspirations. Res. High. Educ. **56**, 813–842 (2015). https://doi.org/10.1007/s11162-015-9375-x
21. Fryer, R.G., Levitt, S.D.: An empirical analysis of the gender gap in mathematics. Am. Econ. J. Appl. Econ. **2**, 210–240 (2010)
22. Cimpian, J.R., Lubienski, S.T., Timmer, J.D., Makowski, M.B., Miller, E.K.: Have gender gaps in math closed? achievement, teacher perceptions, and learning behaviors across two ECLS-K cohorts. AERA Open. **2**, 2332858416673617 (2016). https://doi.org/10.1177/2332858416673617
23. Aronson, E., Wilson, T.D., Akert, R.M.: Social psychology. Pearson Education, Harlow (2014)
24. Garriott, P.O., Hultgren, K.M., Frazier, J.: STEM stereotypes and high school students' math/science career goals. J. Career Assess. **25**, 585–600 (2017). https://doi.org/10.1177/1069072716665825

25. Starr, C.R.: "I'm Not a Science Nerd!": STEM stereotypes, identity, and motivation among undergraduate women. Psychol. Women Q. **42**, 489–503 (2018). https://doi.org/10.1177/036 1684318793848

26. McArthur, B.A., Madigan, S., Korczak, D.J.: Tweens are not teens: the problem of amalgamating broad age groups when making pandemic recommendations. Can. J. Public Health. **112**, 984–987 (2021). https://doi.org/10.17269/s41997-021-00585-6

27. McGuire, L., et al.: Gender stereotypes and peer selection in STEM domains among children and adolescents. Sex Roles **87**, 455–470 (2022). https://doi.org/10.1007/s11199-022-01327-9

28. Kessels, U.: Fitting into the stereotype: How gender-stereotyped perceptions of prototypic peers relate to liking for school subjects. Eur. J. Psychol. Educ. **20**, 309–323 (2005). https://doi.org/10.1007/BF03173559

29. Cheryan, S., Plaut, V.C., Handron, C., Hudson, L.: The stereotypical computer scientist: gendered media representations as a barrier to inclusion for women. Sex Roles **69**, 58–71 (2013). https://doi.org/10.1007/s11199-013-0296-x

30. OECD: Mathematics Self-Beliefs and Participation in Mathematics-Related Activities. OECD, Paris (2013)

31. Clark Blickenstaff, J.: Women and science careers: leaky pipeline or gender filter? Gend. Educ. **17**, 40369–40418 (2005). https://doi.org/10.1080/09540250500145072

32. Atit, K., et al.: Examining the relations between spatial skills and mathematical performance: a meta-analysis. Psychon. Bull. Rev. **29**, 699–720 (2022). https://doi.org/10.3758/s13423-021-02012-w

33. Mejía-Rodríguez, A.M., Luyten, H., Meelissen, M.R.M.: Gender differences in mathematics self-concept across the world: an exploration of student and parent data of TIMSS 2015. Int J of Sci and Math Educ. **19**, 1229–1250 (2021). https://doi.org/10.1007/s10763-020-10100-x

34. Niemivirta, M., Tapola, A., Tuominen, H., Viljaranta, J.: Developmental trajectories of school-beginners' ability self-concept, intrinsic value and performance in mathematics. Bri. J. Educ. Psychol. n/a (2023). https://doi.org/10.1111/bjep.12655

35. Postigo, Á., Fernández-Alonso, R., Fonseca-Pedrero, E., González-Nuevo, C., Muñiz, J.: Academic self-concept dramatically declines in secondary school: personal and contextual determinants. Int. J. Environ. Res. Public Health **19**, 3010 (2022). https://doi.org/10.3390/ijerph19053010

36. Linn, M.C., Petersen, A.C.: Emergence and characterization of sex differences in spatial ability: a meta-analysis. Child Dev. **56**, 1479–1498 (1985). https://doi.org/10.2307/1130467

37. Voyer, D., Voyer, S., Bryden, M.P.: Magnitude of sex differences in spatial abilities: a meta-analysis and consideration of critical variables. Psychol. Bull. **117**, 250–270 (1995)

38. Rahe, M., Ruthsatz, V., Schürmann, L., Quaiser-Pohl, C.: The effects of feedback on the gender differences in the performance in a chronometric mental-rotation test. J. Cogn. Psychol. **31**, 467–475 (2019). https://doi.org/10.1080/20445911.2019.1621872

39. Modroño, C., et al.: Developmental grey matter changes in superior parietal cortex accompany improved transitive reasoning. Think. Reason. **25**, 151–170 (2018). https://doi.org/10.1080/13546783.2018.1481144

40. Peterson, E., Weinberger, A., Uttal, D., Kolvoord, B., Green, A.: Spatial activity participation in childhood and adolescence: consistency and relations to spatial thinking in adolescence. Cogn. Res.-Princ. Impl. **5** (2020). https://doi.org/10.1186/s41235-020-00239-0

41. Quaiser-Pohl, C.: The mental cutting test 'Schnitte' and the picture rotation test-two new measures to assess spatial ability. Int. J. Test. **3**, 219–231 (2003). https://doi.org/10.1207/S15327574IJT0303_2

42. Ruthsatz, V., Neuburger, S., Jansen, P., Quaiser-Pohl, C.: Pellet figures, the feminine answer to cube figures? Influence of stimulus features and rotational axis on the menatl-rotation performance of fourth-grade boys and girls. Spatial Cogn. 370–382 (2014)

43. Ruthsatz, V., Quaiser-Pohl, C.M., Saunders, M., Lennon-Maslin, M.: Male? Female? Neutral! Using Novel Polyhedral Figures as Gender-Neutral Stimuli in a Mental Rotation Test. (forthcoming.)

44. Ruthsatz, V., Neuburger, S., Jansen, P., Quaiser-Pohl, C.: Cars or dolls? Influence of the stereotyped nature of the items on children's mental-rotation performance. Learn. Individ. Differ. **43**, 75–82 (2015). https://doi.org/10.1016/j.lindif.2015.08.016

45. Ehm, J.-H.: Akademisches Selbstkonzept im Grundschulalter. Entwicklungsanalyse dimensionaler Vergleiche und Exploration differenzieller Unterschiede. pedocs (2014)

46. Marsh, H., Byrne, B.M., Shavelson, R.: A multifaceted academic self-concept: its hierarchical structure and its relation to academic achievement. J. Educ. Psychol. **80**, 366–380 (1988). https://doi.org/10.1037/0022-0663.80.3.366

47. Ada Lovelace-Projekt: MINT-Mentoring - Ada-Lovelace-Projekt. https://ada-lovelace.de/mint-mentoring/

48. Space Science Institute: Tweens and STEM (2023). https://www.starnetlibraries.org/resources/tweens-and-stem/

49. Lennon-Maslin, M., Quaiser-Pohl, C.M., Ruthsatz, V., Saunders, M.: Under my skin: reducing bias in STEM through new approaches to assessment of spatial abilities considering the role of emotional regulation. Soc. Sci. **12**, 356 (2023). https://doi.org/10.3390/socsci12060356

50. Saunders, M., Quaiser-Pohl, C.M.: Identifying solution strategies in a mental-rotation test with gender-stereotyped objects by analyzing gaze patterns. J. Eye Move. Res. **13** (2020). https://doi.org/10.16910/jemr.13.6.5

51. Rahe, M., Quaiser-Pohl, C.: Can (perceived) mental-rotation performance mediate gender differences in math anxiety in adolescents and young adults? Math. Ed. Res. J. (2021). https://doi.org/10.1007/s13394-021-00387-6

52. Ramirez, G., Gunderson, E.A., Levine, S.C., Beilock, S.L.: Spatial anxiety relates to spatial abilities as a function of working memory in children. Q. J. Exp. Psychol. **65**, 474–487 (2012). https://doi.org/10.1080/17470218.2011.616214

Eliciting Spatial Reasoning Actions Through Projective Geometry in the Elementary Classroom

Lynn M. McGarvey[1]([✉]) [ID], Josh Markle[1] [ID], and Jennifer S. Thom[2] [ID]

[1] University of Alberta, Edmonton, AB, Canada
{lmcg,jmarkle}@ualberta.ca
[2] University of Victoria, Victoria, BC, Canada
jethom@uvic.ca

Abstract. Spatial thinking is an essential and uniting form of reasoning across science, technology, engineering, and mathematics (STEM). This paper explores projective geometry ideas accessible to elementary school-aged children, specifically focusing on understanding, exploring, and analyzing relationships between 3D objects and their 2D projections. We posit that projective geometry has the potential to elicit spatial reasoning actions, such as visualization, dimension-shifting, and perspective taking, and provides a unifying theme in which to explicitly attend to 2D representations of 3D objects. In the paper, we share three tasks rooted in projective geometry: Moving Shadows, Structured Perspective Drawings, and Design-Build-Draw. We piloted these tasks with children aged 5 to 11, illustrating the spatial actions elicited by the tasks through the children's gestures, responses, drawings, and models.

Keywords: Spatial Reasoning · Projective Geometry · Shadows · Perspective Drawing · 3D Modelling

1 Introduction

Spatial reasoning is ubiquitous in daily life. Interpreting graphs, diagrams, and charts, constructing 3D objects from 2D drawings, and packing boxes and arranging objects efficiently are just a few examples of how we regularly engage with the world in spatial ways. Despite its prominence, many people assume that spatial ability is innate—either you have it or you don't: "I always get disoriented in the mall"; "I'd rather hire someone to assemble flat-pack furniture than attempt to do it myself"; "I will drive five extra blocks than try to parallel park." Despite these claims, we are all spatial beings. Much of our understanding of the world is situated in how we navigate our bodies through space and the embodied ways we interpret and interact with the environments we encounter.

Spatial thinking is an essential and uniting form of reasoning across science, technology, engineering and mathematics (STEM). Spatial ability is associated with mathematics [1] and science achievement [2], success and retention in engineering education [3], and the extent to which students go on to pursue STEM careers [4]. Moreover, there

M. Živković et al. (Eds.): Spatial Cognition 2024, LNAI 14756, pp. 32–47, 2024.
https://doi.org/10.1007/978-3-031-63115-3_3

is mounting evidence suggesting that students respond to spatial interventions [5–9]; yet, spatial ability receives little explicit attention in elementary curricula [10].

Mathematics texts and materials are replete with visual representations, such as graphs, diagrams, and concrete and pictorial models. While these representations are often assumed to carry meaningful information, they are not always explicitly addressed in student learning. In elementary mathematics education, the focus tends to be on number, overshadowing fundamental spatial skills including the spatial aspects of counting, comparing, composing, decomposing, and others. Neglecting the visual-spatial elements in mathematics has long term consequences for student learning.

In a previous project of the Spatial Reasoning Study Group [11], we compared the spatial skills assessed in engineering education with parallel assessments appropriate for children. We noted that the engineering assessments and interventions addressed dynamic spatial skills such as translating between 2D representations and 3D objects, performing rigid transformations through physical and mental rotation, and engaging in dynamic transformations such as paper folding and cross-cutting. Yet, traditional curricula in geometry, an ideal place to offer explicit spatial opportunities, tends to prioritize static, rather than dynamic geometric skills. To address this gap and create a dynamic space for spatial learning, our research team explored the potential of projective geometry to elicit spatial reasoning actions in the elementary classroom. Projective geometry plays a critical role in various fields such as modelling light rays and shadows in science, creating technical drawings for 3D structures in engineering, and designing computer graphics to render realistic 3D scenes on 2D screens. It also offers an alternative approach to studying geometric shapes, spaces, and properties in mathematics. Below, we provide a description of projective geometry along with three extended classroom-based tasks piloted with children, demonstrating the potential of projective geometry to foster spatial reasoning actions in the elementary mathematics classroom.

2 What is Projective Geometry

Historically, projective geometry grew out of efforts of artists and architects to represent or project the 3D world onto a flat surface. It rose to prominence during the Renaissance through the works of architect Filippo Brunelleschi (1377–1446), and artists Leon Battista Alberti (1404–1472) and Masaccio (1401–1428). In the 19th-century, mathematicians such as Jean-Victor Poncelet (1788–1867) further developed the field as a distinct branch of mathematics. Today, projective geometry is typically only studied at the post-secondary level through the exploration of Desargue's, Pappas's, and Pascal's theorems (see Dynamic Projective Geometry visualizations) [12].

Projective geometry differs from the Euclidean geometry traditionally taught in school mathematics. While Euclidean geometry is concerned with measurable attributes, such as angle and length, projective geometry focuses on the relationships between elemental geometric objects including points, lines, and planes. While Euclidean geometry employs tools like ruler and compass, projective geometry relies on a straight edge, illustrating its apparent simplicity despite its underlying complexity. The complexity of projective geometry becomes apparent when considering our everyday experiences. For example, imagine standing on railroad tracks and observing how they seem to converge at the horizon (see Fig. 1). We know the rails are parallel, but how do we reconcile our understanding with our perceptual experience of them seeming to join together at a point on the horizon? Projective geometry offers the tools to explore this confluence of geometric space and perceptual experience. Consider a second thought experiment. Imagine the point where the railroad tracks appear to converge. Now imagine sliding that point to the left and right along the horizon; notice how the tracks, which appear to converge at that point, shift accordingly. This movement of the "point at infinity" reflects how parallel lines adjust in a perspective drawing.

Fig. 1. Parallel lines in real life (image: stock.adobe.com/nordroden).

There is a radical, but taken for granted, shift in thinking required to reconcile a Euclidean representation of the world and a visual projection of that world. In elementary school, when studying common 3D shapes (see Fig. 2), the projected images deviate from our expectations. For example, the projected image of the cube has both obtuse and acute angles instead of the expected right angles at its vertices; and the top of the cylinder is projected as an ellipse, rather than a circle. Projective geometry provides opportunities to study the dynamic relationships between 3D objects and their 2D projections.

Fig. 2. Projections of 3D geometric objects studied in elementary school (image: Freepik.com).

3 Projective Geometry Tasks in the Classroom

In the 1950s and 60s, Piaget and Inhelder [13] contended that prior to understanding Euclidean relations, emphasizing distance, angle, and properties of shapes, children first develop an understanding of topological relations, involving proximity, relative position, enclosure, and continuity. Subsequently, they progress to projective relations, including position, orientation, and relationships of objects in space from different perspectives. This hypothesis sparked educational research exploring the potential of projective geometry in the classroom. For example, Lesh [14] wrote:

> Few mathematical topics can compare with the simplicity, power, and elegant beauty of projective geometry, and few mathematical topics are so firmly rooted in concrete experience; yet, few laboratory activities have been developed to exploit the intuitive origins of projective geometry. [14, p. 202]

We also believe that there are tremendous opportunities to explore spatial reasoning through the concrete and dynamic aspects of projective geometry. However, despite its potential, research into projective geometry with children was abandoned and remains largely absent from elementary school curricula, with few tasks, resources, and literature available [15]. Nearly 40 years ago, Mansfield [16] authored one of the few articles explicitly mentioning projective geometry. She described a series of seven lessons using light and shadow to investigate the relationships between objects and their projections (i.e., shadows). While Mansfield acknowledged the importance of such geometric investigations for developing spatial skills, she noted that these tasks "may be difficult to find or difficult to teach, or they may not be seen as important activities in their own right" [16, p. 16].

Explicit references to projective geometry in mathematics education literature are rare [e.g., 17]. Instead, projective ideas are often implicit in education-based literature. For example, Lee and Kurz [18] proposed an activity investigating the relationship between shadows and the sun's position in the sky, an analogy that was brought forth by students in the shadow task we describe below. However, Lee and Kurz were more focused on data collection and organization than geometric concepts. Similarly, Clark and Clark [19] included shadow tasks as part of their investigation of conic sections. While their ideas attended to projective ideas, they focused on middle and secondary school learning outcomes. Other articles involving elementary-age students assess students' 3D visualization skills through perspective and orthogonal drawings [e.g., 20, 21], but they do not explicitly reference projective geometry making it difficult to compile relevant literature on the topic. Our aim here is to present classroom-tested tasks that use ideas from projective geometry and have the potential to elicit spatial actions from elementary school students.

4 Framework for Conceptualizing Spatial Actions

Our task development and discussion are guided by the view that spatial reasoning is a complex process in which learners engage in acts of "orienting, decomposing/recomposing, shifting dimensions, balancing, diagramming…feeling, and visualizing," among others [22, p. 140]. We draw on Davis et al.'s circular diagram of Spatial Actions (see Fig. 3) as a framework for conceptualizing and analyzing the engagement of learners.[1] The Spatial Actions diagram allows us to identify and articulate distinct elements of spatial reasoning, such as symmetrizing and comparing, while emphasizing that such actions rarely occur in isolation. That is, each learner may blend and extend spatial actions uniquely while engaged in activity, and different learners may use different spatial actions for the same task. Therefore, rather than designing tasks to target specific skills, we use the Spatial Actions framework to observe student engagement and analyze the opportunities for spatial actions within the tasks developed. This approach allows us to understand how learners interact with spatial concepts and apply them in various contexts.

5 Task Design and Implementation

In this section, we present three tasks designed to emphasize projective geometry ideas that elicit dynamic spatial reasoning actions including, Moving Shadows, Structured Perspective Drawings, and Design-Draw-Build. In the Moving Shadows task, we explore projective ideas through an investigation into the relationships between geometric objects and their varying shadows on a plane. This task leverages transformations between 3D objects and 2D projections, prompting students to observe how projections shift with movement. The Structured Perspective Drawings task challenges students to grapple with the spatial discrepancy between 2D shapes on a page, and the 2D shapes created

---

[1] The image in Davis et al. [22, p. 141] shown in Fig. 3 is described, but only named as "the diagram" in the text. We refer to it as the Spatial Actions diagram or framework.

Fig. 3. Davis et al.'s [22, p. 141] Spatial Actions framework. Used with permission.

by projecting 3D objects onto a 2D surface. It provides a structured approach to creating perspective drawings, encouraging students to confront the complexities of translating 3D objects onto a 2D plane. Lastly, the Design- Build-Draw task involves designing and representing a 3D cube structure within given constraints, first with technology, then by constructing a physical model, and finally by creating technical drawings. This task also underscores the relationship between 3D objects and 2D representations, emphasizing the process of translating concrete objects into tangible designs and drawings.

5.1 Participants

Our task design and analysis encompassed two phases of data collection involving two different groups of elementary school-aged children. In the first phase, we invited children via their parents to help us assess the appropriateness of new geometry tasks for elementary school. Fourteen children (5 female; 9 male), aged five to eleven years old, participated in three online sessions (via Zoom), each lasting approximately 45 to 60 mins. The activity sessions took place in the participants' homes, either individually or in pairs with siblings or friends. In the second phase, we modified previously developed tasks and created new ones tailored to specific grade levels. These tasks were implemented in four classrooms (grades 2, 3, 4, and 5) in two elementary schools over a two-year period. Sixty-eight students (32 female; 36 male) worked on the tasks in groups of three or four. The tasks were implemented over a series of eighteen 50-minute lessons per grade throughout the school year.

In this paper we showcase three tasks developed and implemented with the participants. The first task, Moving Shadows, was introduced in a Grade 5 classroom and we present the experiences of one group of three students. The second task, Structured Perspective Drawings, draws on the responses of several children from the online activity sessions. The final task, Design-Build-Draw, features the responses of an 8-year-old participant who engaged in the online data collection sessions. All names are anonymized throughout the paper.

Our focus lies in analyzing the forms of spatial reasoning actions elicited by the tasks, rather than assessing individual performance. The data gathered will aid in refining the tasks as part of the ongoing task development project. In this paper we describe the tasks and provide brief analyses of the children's spatial engagement with the tasks based on Davis et al.'s [22] Spatial Actions framework.

6 Task Descriptions and Children's Spatial Engagement

6.1 Moving Shadows

The Moving Shadows task employs projective geometry ideas by investigating how 3D objects are projected onto a 2D surface. In projective geometry, the concept of projection involves representing objects in space onto a plane or surface through the extension of lines from a point-source. In the Moving Shadows task, the flashlight serves as the point-source of light, emitting rays that project the shadows of a geometric solid onto a whiteboard, which acts as the projection plane. By manipulating the position of the flashlight and observing the resulting shadows, students can explore how changes in the position and orientation of the light source affect the shape, size, and position of the shadows on the whiteboard; thus, experimenting with the variant and invariant relationships between 3D objects and their 2D projections.

This Moving Shadows task was implemented in three parts with students in Grade 5. We used a rectangular prism, and a flashlight to cast shadows onto a small, portable whiteboard. In the three parts, the location of the whiteboard and the 3D object stay the same; however, we change the location and path of the light source. The focus is on predicting and investigating how the projection changes and stays the same along the three different light source paths. In all three parts, students were prompted to predict the shape and position of the object's shadow through gestures, verbal descriptions, and sketches. The whiteboard enabled students to draw and later directly compare their predictions with the actual projections.

Figure 4 depicts the set up for the first stage. We placed markers labelled L (left), C (centre), and R (right) in a straight line parallel to the whiteboard. This arrangement ensures that the path of the light source or point-source is parallel to the whiteboard as the projected plane.

In this arrangement, the 3D object and projection surface are fixed but the distance to the light source varies. Several observations can be made. For example, the shadow continues to be comprised of straight lines; as the light source moves to the right, the shadow moves to the left, and vice versa; and, the size of the shadow changes as the distance between the light source and whiteboard varies.

In the second stage of the Moving Shadows task, we created a curved path for the point-source constructed from cardboard (see Fig. 5). Again, we marked points L, C, and R for clarity. After generating and documenting their predictions, we prompted students

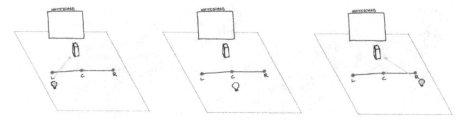

Fig. 4. The point-source slides along a path parallel to the projection surface.

to notice what was variant (e.g., the stretching or skewing of the projection) and invariant (e.g., the preservation of straightness between the 3D object and its 2D projection). In the third and final stage, we asked students to hold the cardboard arc perpendicular to the table with its base parallel to the whiteboard, and to repeat the investigation.

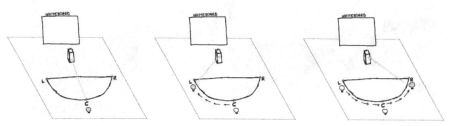

Fig. 5. The point-source slides along a circular path at a different distance from projection surface.

Here we recount an episode with one small group of Grade 5 students engaged in the second stage of the investigation. That is, the circular arc of the light source is laid flat on the table, as depicted in Fig. 5. From the standpoint of projective geometry, our intent was to draw students' noticing to which aspects varied and which were consistent across different projections. Figure 6 shows images of the teacher introducing the curved path followed by part of the ensuing conversation with a group of Grade 5 students. The teacher asks the students to make predictions about the shadows initially.

Teacher: What do you think is going to happen [to the object's shadow] as I follow along the curve [tracing the path of the light source (image a)]?

Ari: It's going to get smaller.

Teacher: It's going to get smaller?

Ari: When it's in the centre [pointing to centre position on the path (image b)], it's going to get smaller. But when it's at the left [pointing to the left side of arc (image c)], it's going to be the same size as that [pointing to the shadow on the whiteboard created with the light source on the right (images d and e)].

Teacher: How come?

Ari: Because these are the same distance [pointing to the left and right sides of the arc]. But this is different [pointing to the centre of the arc]. It's way farther.

The teacher then moves the flashlight along the arc from right to the left, and the students make their observations as the shadow changes.

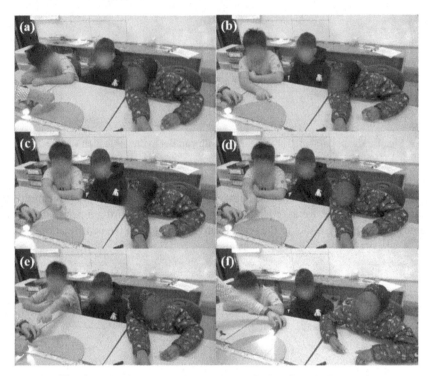

Fig. 6. Ari, Ethan, and Nala working on the Moving Shadows task.

Teacher: So is it getting smaller like you said?
All: Yes!
Teacher: It's changing shape like it did last time, but it's getting smaller, smaller, smaller-
Nala: Skinnier! Skinnier. It's getting skinnier [image f].

The Moving Shadows task elicited a range of spatial actions among the Grade 5 students. As demonstrated by the group shown in Fig. 6 and using the Spatial Actions framework from Fig. 3, we can make several observations of the students' spatial actions. Ari visualized the projection at point R and contrasted it to his prediction at point C, anticipating that it is "going to get smaller." When prompted to provide a rationale, Ari conjectured that there would be symmetry between the projections at points L and R ("these are the same"), but because point C is "way farther," then the projection would become smaller. While all three students appeared to agree that the shadow would "get smaller," likely meaning smaller in height as the point-source approached point C, it was Nala who noticed some variant and invariant qualities of the transformation. She noted that the shadow's width gets "skinnier," but the height remained relatively constant.

6.2 Structured Perspective Drawings

The Structured Perspective Drawings task, adapted from Salisbury [23], explores a range of projective geometry ideas as children investigate how lines and shapes on a page compare with shapes made by the 2D projections of 3D objects on the same page. This task involves a foundational aspect of projective geometry: generating perspective drawings. It focuses on how objects are perceived when projected onto a plane from different viewpoints. The task fosters children's ability to visualize and understand how the lines and shapes in drawings can represent a 3D structure, and once again explore the relationship between 3D objects and their 2D projections.

The task highlights the implicit and potentially erroneous assumption that children visually interpret pictures, graphs, and diagrams appearing in texts, posters, and tests as intended without explicit instruction. However, such images do little to help and can potentially confuse children if they perceive them differently than anticipated. The Structured Perspective Drawing task is designed to draw explicit attention to the relationship and possible discrepancies between a 3D object and its 2D projection or drawing.

The version of this task presented in this paper is based on and illustrated by the group of online participants aged 5 to 11 years old. In this task, the children were presented with a page with three-line segments (Fig. 7a). They were asked to describe what they saw and identify the longest of the three lines. Not surprisingly, the children confidently stated that the middle line was the longest, the left line as the shortest, and some children also noted that the lines were drawn vertically and were parallel. Once 'seeing' the image as three lines, the children were asked to connect the line segments at the top and bottom (Fig. 7b), and then asked what they saw. Responses varied, with some children seeing objects such as, "an ice cream cone," "a diamond," "a box," and occasionally a "rectangular prism." The teacher then asked them to draw a "wavy horizontal line" from either side of the image, sharing an illustration of the intended result (Fig. 7c). Again, the children were asked what they saw. Many children now perceived "a house" or "shed," and for those who did not, the teacher asked, "Could it be a building?" Nearly all learners agreed and pointed to the "walls" and the "sky" and "grass" created by the horizontally sketched lines.

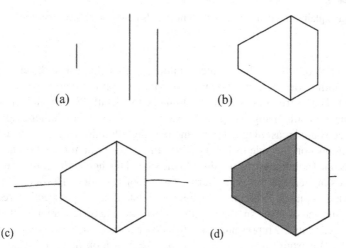

Fig. 7. Three line segments (a); connecting line segments (b); drawing a horizon (c); and identifying the shape of the wall (d).

Once they recognized a building image, the children were asked how many faces or walls they could see and why we could only see two walls. Bella (age 6) illustrated her understanding through spatial actions such as perspective-taking, visualizing, interpreting diagrams, and imagined movement, explaining, "Because you would have to turn. You would have to see the back to see a wall [turns paper over] and that wouldn't work."

Showing the image with one of the visible walls coloured in pink (Fig. 7c), the teacher asks, "What shape is the pink wall?" While many children said, "a rectangle," the teacher probed further, asking, "Does it look like a rectangle?" "How do you know it's a rectangle?" and "Why do you think it looks different?" The children offered a variety of hesitant explanations, such as "it doesn't look the same as real life, but it's still a rectangle" or "if you stand here [pointing to a spot in front of the wall] it would look like a rectangle." The teacher asked, "Which line is the longest now?" As Liam (age 9) explained, "They are both the exact same. Because ... from different angles. See my hands? If I spread it away it looks smaller" (see Fig. 8).

Fig. 8. Liam explains and demonstrates with his hands how when objects get further away, they get smaller.

After completing the outline of their building, the teacher asked the children to add details, including a door, three windows, and two trees approximately the same height as the building. The instructions were to try to make the details "look right" or "realistic." Creating these details using perspective was anticipated to be challenging, but most children used spatial reasoning to create and interpret their drawings. When asked about his two windows on the side of his building (Fig. 9a), William (age 11) said, "Well, I thought this one [pointing to the window on the side of the house closer to the door] looks closer. So it's bigger. But this one is farther, so it looks smaller." Despite both windows being drawn as squares, William applied his understanding of perspective, recognizing that objects further away are smaller. Noah (age 9) articulated the spatial conflict between a 3D building and its 2D representation when describing his windows (Fig. 9a). "I made them square. But from this point of view they kind of look like a rectangle, but then it goes in on two sides [that the ninety-degree angle is not maintained]. ... Because I thought that if I just drew it as a normal square, that would mean that it was doing the opposite of what I did." That is, if he drew a square, in real life the windows would get wider on the sides, rather narrower like in his drawing.

Fig. 9. William's (a) and Noah's (b) structured perspective drawings.

The Structured Perspective Drawing tasks engaged children in a range of actions and reasoning across many parts of the Spatial Actions framework including perspective-taking, visualizing, dimension-shifting, locating, orienting, diagramming, comparing, and relating.

6.3 Design-Build-Draw

The Design-Build-Draw task is a multifaceted activity that integrates technology, engineering, and mathematics, with a focus on projective geometry ideas. Central to this task is the use of computer-aided design (CAD) software, which allows for the "design" of digital representations of 3D structures. CAD software generates a 2D orthographic or projected image of a 3D virtual model which the user can view from different perspectives. The "build" component of the task involves transforming the rendered computer image to a 3D structure. In the final "draw" phase of the task, is the transformation from the 3D concrete model to 2D technical drawings including orthogonal front-side-top views and perspective drawings.

To illustrate the projective and spatial aspects of the task, we share the images, structures, and drawings created by 8-year-old Isaiah during one of his online sessions. In the first phase of the task, children were asked to design a castle using the virtual 3D modelling tool, Tinkercad (see tinkercad.com). Tinkercad is a free and user-friendly digital design application with multiple features. Children were given the following castle design constraints: They may use up to 30 regular building blocks; the structure's footprint should not exceed 12 square blocks; and the highest point could be no more than five blocks tall. Figure 10 illustrates Isaiah's virtual design from three different viewpoints. Isaiah's castle meets the constraints of the task as it uses 30 blocks, has a footprint of 12 square blocks including the overhand; and has a height of four blocks at its highest point.

Once Isaiah was satisfied with his virtual castle, he was given linking cubes and asked to construct a physical replica and ensure that it was both structurally sound when placed

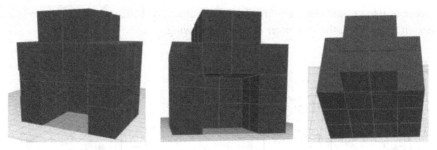

Fig. 10. 3D Design of castle from different angles using Tinkercad.

on a surface, and met the task constraints (see Fig. 11). We asked Isaiah to compare the virtual model with the physical model to ensure they were the same. Isaiah rotated the Tinkercad image and concrete model to the right side, back, and left side simultaneously confirming each time they were the same by describing the height and width of the models.

Fig. 11. Isaiah building a concrete model of a castle and confirming the number of blocks used.

Finally, Isaiah produced different technical drawings based on his physical model (Fig. 12). In the first set of drawings, he was asked to imagine shining a flashlight on the front of his castle and drawing what he thought the shadow would look like. This instruction was similar to a task done in a previous session. He was also asked to create both a right view and top view using a similar process of shining a light on those surfaces (Fig. 12a). Finally, he was asked to create a perspective drawing by placing the right front edge forward, drawing the vertical line created, and completing the drawing from that viewpoint. Again, this was similar to a previous session on creating perspective drawings—an extension of the Structured Perspective Drawing task above. Here, Isaiah oriented both the physical and the Tinkercad drawing with the right front edge forward. Isaiah initially used his concrete model to draw, but then focused mainly on the 2D Tinkercad model to create the perspective drawing (Fig. 12b).

Isaiah's work to design, build, and draw a castle reveals many different forms of spatial activity embedded within the projective geometry task. Isaiah composed, arranged, and fitted the 30 linking cubes together; he interpreted the 2D images generated in the

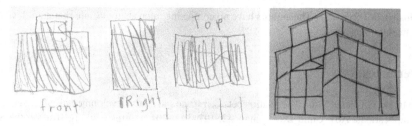

Fig. 12. Front-side-top view (a) and perspective drawing of a castle (b).

digital model to create a 3D structure; he located and oriented both the 2D projection and 3D model in similar ways, and he engaged in perspective-taking in order to produce technical drawings that were 2D projections of a 3D model.

7 Concluding Remarks

This paper highlights the significant, yet underexplored potential of projective geometry in enhancing spatial reasoning among elementary students in a mathematics classroom. It demonstrates how projective geometry can bridge practical visual experiences with more abstract mathematical ideas. The tasks described—Moving Shadows, Structured Perspective Drawings, and Design-Build-Draw—illustrate a few of the concrete ways in which projective geometry ideas can foster critical spatial actions. The opportunities offered by the tasks were illustrated with gestures, drawings, and responses offered by elementary school-aged children aged five to eleven. As anticipated, the tasks were rich with opportunities to both engage in spatial actions, such as dimension-shifting, visualizing, and perspective-taking.

Highlighting multi-layered spatial actions as emphasized in Davis et al. [22] Spatial Actions framework (see Fig. 3), we observed students altering, situating, sensating, and moving as they investigated shadow paths, perspective drawings, and designing, constructing and drawing 3D-structures. Importantly, by attending to spatial processes beyond what is explicitly addressed in curriculum learning outcomes, students were asked to meaningfully attend to the similarities and differences between 3D objects and their 2D representations, and to note the discrepancies occurring between what appears on a page and their real-life perceptual experiences. The tasks also integrated mathematics with technology, science, and engineering, and, as well, made connections to other disciplines such as art. The three tasks and students' responses to those tasks point to projective geometry as a rich source of mathematical inquiry in the elementary school and its potential to elicit spatial reasoning actions.

The study challenges traditional views of geometry education by shifting the focus from static geometry to dynamic spatial skills, crucial for understanding and manipulating 3D objects and their 2D representations. Projective geometry offers ideas accessible to younger learners through which to engage with dynamic spatial skills known to support mathematics achievement.

Acknowledgments. This study was funded by the Social Sciences and Humanities Research Council of Canada.

Disclosure of Interests. The authors have no competing interests to declare that are relevant to the content of this article.

References

1. Mix, K,S., Cheng, Y.-L.: The relation between space and math: developmental and educational implications. Adv. Child Dev. Behav. **42**, 197–243 (2012). https://doi.org/10.1016/B978-0-12-394388-0.00006-X
2. Hodgkiss, A., Gilligan, K.A., Tolmie, A.K., Thomas, M.S.C., Farran, E.K.: Spatial cognition and science achievement: the contribution of intrinsic and extrinsic spatial skills from 7 to 11 Years. Br. J. Educ. Psychol. **88**(4), 675–697 (2018). https://doi.org/10.1111/bjep.12211
3. Sorby, S.A., Baartmans, B.J.: The development and assessment of a course for enhancing the 3-D spatial visualization skills of first year engineering students. J. Eng. Educ. **89**(3), 301–307 (2000). https://doi.org/10.1002/j.2168-9830.2000.tb00529.x
4. Wai, J., Lubinski, D., Benbow, C.P.: Spatial ability for STEM domains: aligning over 50 years of cumulative psychological knowledge solidifies its importance. J. Educ. Psychol. **101**(4), 817–835 (2009). https://doi.org/10.1037/a0016127
5. Gilligan-Lee, K.A., Hawes, Z.C.K., Mix, K.S.: Spatial thinking as the missing piece in mathematics curricula. NPJ Sci. Learn. **7**(10) (2022). https://doi.org/10.1038/s41539-022-00128-9
6. Hawes, Z.C.K., Gilligan-Lee, K.A., Mix, K.: Effects of spatial training on mathematics performance: a meta-analysis. Dev. Psychol. **58**(1), 112–137 (2022). https://doi.org/10.1037/dev0001281
7. Mix, K.S., Levine, S.C., Cheng, Y.-L., Stockton, J.D., Bower, C.: Effects of spatial training on mathematics in first and sixth grade children. J. Educ. Psychol. **113**(2), 304–314 (2021). https://doi.org/10.1037/edu0000494
8. Uttal, D.H., et al.: The malleability of spatial skills: a meta-analysis of training studies. Psychol. Bull. **139**(2), 352–402 (2013). https://doi.org/10.1037/a0028446
9. Verdine, B.N., Golinkoff, R.M., Hirsh-Pasek, K., Newcombe, N.S.: Finding the missing piece: blocks, puzzles, and shapes fuel school readiness. Trends Neurosci. Educ. **3**(1), 7–13 (2014). https://doi.org/10.1016/j.tine.2014.02.005
10. Sinclair, N., Bruce, C.D.: New opportunities in geometry education at the primary school. ZDM Math. Educ. **47**, 319–329 (2015). https://doi.org/10.1007/s11858-015-0693-4
11. McGarvey, L., Luo, L., Hawes, Z.: Spatial reasoning study group: spatial skills framework for young engineers. In: English, L., Moore, T. (eds.) Early engineering learning, pp. 53–81. Springer (2018)
12. McGarvey, M.J.: Desmos classroom: projective geometry (n.d.). https://teacher.desmos.com/activitybuilder/custom/651f1dfde55dfb2c13e68bc8
13. Piaget, J., Inhelder, B.: The child's conception of space. Routledge & Kegan Paul (1967)
14. Lesh, R.: Transformational geometry in elementary school: Some research issues. In: Martin, J. L., David, A. (eds.) Space and Geometry. Papers from a Research Workshop, pp. 185–243. Ohio State University (1976)
15. McGarvey, L.M., Thom, J.S., Markle, J.: Creating space for a topic in the null curriculum. In: Thompson, D., Huntley, M.A., Suurtamm, C. (eds.) Lessons learned from research on mathematics curriculum. Information Age Publishing (in press)
16. Mansfield, H.: Projective geometry in the elementary school. Arith. Teach. **32**(7), 15–19 (1985)
17. Salisbury, A. J.: Projective geometry in the primary school curriculum: Children's spatial-perceptual abilities. Doctoral Dissertation, University of London (1983)

18. Lee, M.Y., Kurz, T.L.: Lights, shadow, action! Teach. Child. Math. **24**(2), 136–138 (2017)
19. Clark, J., Clark, J. M.: Hands-on conics worked for me. Math. Teach. Learn. Teach. PK-**113**(7), 573–80 (2020). https://doi.org/10.5951/MTLT.2019.0010
20. Pittalis, M., Christou, C.: Coding and decoding representations of 3D shapes. J. Math. Behav. **32**(3), 673–689 (2013). https://doi.org/10.1016/j.jmathb.2013.08.004
21. Sack, J.J.: Development of a top-view numeric coding teaching-learning trajectory within an elementary grades 3-D visualization design research project. J. Math. Behav. **32**(2), 183–196 (2013). https://doi.org/10.1016/j.jmathb.2013.02.006
22. Davis, B.: Spatial reasoning study group: spatial reasoning in the early years: principles, assertions, and speculations. Routledge (2015)
23. Salisbury, A.J.: Primary school geometry: some unusual activities. Int. J. Math. Educ. Sci. Technol. **18**(3), 471–478 (1987). https://doi.org/10.1080/0020739870180319

Gender Differences

Gender in Teacher-Student Interactions: Another Factor in Spatial Ability Development and STEM Affiliation

Gamarra Estefania[✉], Tenbrink Thora, and Mills Debra

Bangor University, Bangor, UK
{e.gamarraburga,t.tenbrink,d.l.mills}@bangor.ac.uk

Abstract. This study explores gender dynamics in teacher-student interactions during a route planning task in science classes, examining six classes—three in Year 5 (ages 8–9) and three in Year 6 (ages 10–11) —in an English-medium international school in the Netherlands. According to the literature, these specific years mark a notable shift in children's gender identity development, such as in relation to male-dominated fields. Our findings indicate a corresponding shift in teacher-student dynamics, with teachers exhibiting prioritised interaction with boys in Year 6 but not 5. The most pronounced difference surfaces in the form of positive feedback, with girls receiving substantially less reinforcement in Year 6. Importantly, these altered teacher-student interactions do not align with gender differences in spatial abilities as measured by relevant spatial tests. However, girls in Year 6 participated less and assumed leadership roles in the activity less frequently. This suggests a potential impact of internalised gender stereotypes on girls' assertiveness and engagement in the classroom, which teacher-student interactions might reinforce. Our findings highlight the complex interplay of gender biases, teacher-student interactions, student engagement, and performance on spatial tasks, offering implications for educators aiming to cultivate equitable and inclusive learning environments.

Keywords: Gender differences · feedback · spatial task performance

1 Introduction

In the quest for equitable education, educators and researchers hope to create biasfree learning environments. However, gender stereotypes are deeply internalised as part of society and culture, and not all of their effects are obvious to the casual observer. This study investigates the complex interplay of internalised gender biases within teacher-student interactions, exploring their impact on spatial abilities and performance. It aims to trace any effects of a known shift in children's gender development around age 10 to see if there may be a corresponding observable difference in classroom dynamics.

Previous studies have demonstrated that around the age of ten is a crucial time for the emergence of gender differences in spatial ability [25]. It has also been shown that it is around this age that children start consolidating their gender identity [28] and

M. Živković et al. (Eds.): Spatial Cognition 2024, LNAI 14756, pp. 51–65, 2024.
https://doi.org/10.1007/978-3-031-63115-3_4

internalising all the cultural assumptions that come with it [18]. This study seeks to augment the existing literature by elucidating the nuanced role of gender in teacher-student interactions and, subsequently, delineating the potential impact of these interactions on students' academic performance.

By unravelling these dynamics, the study aims not only to enhance our understanding of gender biases in education but also to guide interventions that foster equitable spatial skill development and task performance among students.

2   Literature Review

2.1   Gender and Gender Differences in Spatial Cognition

Traditionally, gender is viewed as a social construct that derives from biological sex, shaping societal expectations regarding the characteristics, behaviours, and attitudes associated with men and women [9]. While gender is a social construct influenced by societal perspectives, individuals play an active role in shaping their gender identity by either conforming to or rejecting societal norms [7]. In consequence, gender develops throughout the lifespan because societies and individuals are constantly changing.

One of the areas where clear gender differences have been found is spatial cognition [14], which is considered an essential ability for success in STEM careers [36]. According to the literature, gender differences in spatial ability usually favour boys and men (e.g., [17, 24, 25]). However, there is abundant evidence that spatial ability is malleable [37], for instance, by successful interventions to close the gap [35]. Interestingly, gender differences in spatial ability are not consistently observed before approximately ten years of age [12, 21, 25], a critical period for social identity formation [33]. Moreover, the absence of compelling evidence linking prenatal androgens to spatial ability [6] challenges assumptions regarding the innate determination of this skill and associated gender differences. Furthermore, meta-analytic investigations have cast doubt on the explanatory power of other biological factors, including hormonal influences, genetics, and brain lateralisation, in accounting for these differences [2]. These findings underscore the potential significance of environmental factors in shaping spatial abilities.

2.2   Gender in the Classroom

Adopting a dynamic concept of gender implies that in the classroom, teachers may adjust their behaviour based on their perceptions of students' gender, and students, in turn, might act in alignment with the gender identity they assert. Several studies show how gender plays a significant role in guiding these interactions.

Teachers' Attention
Much evidence demonstrates that teachers divide their attention differently based on the gender of their students [11, 29, 32]. Studies conducted in math or science classrooms found that teachers tended to praise boys more often, gave them more informative feedback [29] and asked them more questions [11]. Others found that teachers tend to pay more attention to boys in general [4, 30] even when they believe they are paying more

attention to girls [40]. Whyte's [40] study stands out for its focus on addressing attention imbalance between genders through an intervention.

Notably, in interviews with teachers who successfully achieved a balance in attention, they reported a perceptual shift - they now felt that they were paying more attention to girls than boys. This discrepancy between teachers' self-perception and the actual classroom dynamics echoes a study by Sunderland [32] where teachers claimed in interviews to be providing more or equal attention to girls, but when their classrooms were observed, the reality proved otherwise.

Gender Stereotypes

Gender stereotypes are "assumptions about what females and males are like, as well as what they ought to be like" [14, p. 237]. These assumptions can guide interactions and influence performance [11].

Many authors now agree that around the age of ten is a critical period for the emergence of significant gender differences in spatial ability [12, 21, 34]. It is also around this age that children become more conscious of their gender identity [28] and begin internalising gender stereotypes [18]. This convergence of factors amplifies the impact of gender stereotypes on children's interests [22], as well as their attention and retention patterns [16]. In consequence, children's activities, interests, and emerging skills become more divided along gender lines.

In a classroom setting, the emergence of *stereotype threats* has the potential to adversely affect the performance of groups subjected to negative stereotypes [19]. Specifically, a *stereotype threat* occurs when a group is burdened by negative stereotypes, leading to a detrimental impact on their performance in tasks associated with those stereotypes [31]. Given the well-established stereotype that "boys are better at maths and science than girls" [3], even the mere acknowledgement that a task is associated with these subjects could potentially trigger a stereotype threat scenario. Thus, the way in which a teacher introduces a task and engages with students during task development is crucial, particularly in subjects characterised by prevalent gender stereotypes, such as STEM disciplines. Teacher-student interactions that perpetuate and reinforce gender stereotypes will impact academic performance [11, 20] – and ultimately, such stereotypes can shape students' future career choices, especially in STEM [10].

2.3 Gender and STEM

Many researchers have attempted to explain the gender gap in STEM. Hughes et al. [15] classified these reasons into two categories: "supply-side" and "demand-side". Within the supply-side category, studies attribute the gender gap in STEM to gender disparities in motivations and abilities. Conversely, arguments placing the root cause of the gap on structural aspects of STEM faculty or the work environment fall under the demand-side category. Studies on spatial abilities fall under supply-side analyses, whereas investigations into classroom dynamics are classified as demand-side analyses. Focusing on education, the demand-side gap starts at school and continues into higher education. In school, it has already been discussed how teachers' actions could reinforce gender stereotypes and how this can affect students' career choices.

Additionally, various studies have identified systemic factors exacerbating the gender gap. These include the exclusion of women from networking events crucial for career advancement [41], the presence of gender-biased processes in hiring or promotions [15], and the prevalence of gender stereotypes shaping how professors perceive their students' performance [38].

Effectively addressing the gender gap in STEM necessitates a comprehensive approach that concurrently targets the issue's demand-side and supply-side aspects. Interventions addressing the development of spatial abilities exemplify strategies for the supply side, while interventions fostering awareness of gender stereotypes exemplify strategies for the demand side. The present study concentrates on the demand side within the school context by examining teachers' discourse and interactions with students in a science class during a navigation task. The primary objective of this analysis is to ascertain whether the gender of their students influences teachers' actions and to discern the potential repercussions of such influences on students' performance in the classroom at the critical age when significant gender differences in spatial abilities and inclination towards STEM start to appear.

3 Methods

3.1 Participants

Six British science teachers, three from Year 5 (two women, one man), and three from Year 6 (two women, one man) agreed to participate in this study. All of them were teachers in an international English-medium private school that follows the British curricula located outside of the United Kingdom.

One hundred and fifteen students ages eight to nine (Year five; $M = 9.02$) and ten to eleven (Year 6; $M = 10.19$). The children had different nationalities, but 51.28% reported speaking English at home. The school was completely English medium, so 100% of the students spoke English at school, with more than 90% reporting using English to communicate with their friends (Table 1).

Table 1. Number of students per class

Class	girls	boys	Other
5.1	7	10	1
5.2	6	8	1
5.3	9	8	
6.1	9	11	1
6.2	9	13	
6.3	10	12	
total	50	62	3

3.2 Materials

Test and Questionnaires

The children were handed a questionnaire designed to collect demographic information and gather details about their familiarity with using maps and engaging in spatial activities. The Spatial-Reasoning Instrument [27] was employed to gauge the children's proficiency in mental rotation and spatial visualisation. Subsequently, an independent t-test was conducted to ascertain potential gender disparities within each class and across each school year using children's individual scores. The results, detailed in Table 2 for reference, indicate that only one class (5.3) exhibited significant differences favouring boys for both mental rotation and spatial visualisation components. However, when assessing gender differences across all three classes within each school year, no significant differences were observed.

Table 2. Spatial-reasoning instrument results by gender

Class	MR girls average	MR boys average	t-test result	SV girls average	SV boys average	t-test result
5.1	3.7	6.1	$p = .089$	2.9	4.1	$p = .228$
5.2	5.5	4.8	$p = .660$	3.8	3.4	$p = .694$
5.3	4	6.9	$p = .005$	2.8	5	$p = .023$
6.1	5.3	5.9	$p = .651$	3.6	4.6	$p = .181$
6.2	5.1	4.8	$p = .700$	5.1	4.2	$p = .236$
6.3	4.5	5.8	$p = .348$	3.8	4.9	$p = .327$

The teachers were given a questionnaire eliciting demographic background as well as teachers' perceptions of their students. Specifically, teachers were presented with open-ended questions prompting them to express their expectations regarding which students they believed would excel in the task and which ones they anticipated might encounter challenges. This aspect of the questionnaire aimed to explore whether teachers might have conscious biases, particularly concerning gender, given the nature of the task involving navigation.

The Task

Teachers were provided digital and hard copies of a tourist map made for children. The instructions accompanying the map directed the children to plan a route that included stops at three specific destinations before concluding at the city museum. Teachers were instructed to exercise flexibility and adapt the activity as appropriate. It was emphasised that while the approach could vary, the overarching objective should remain consistent: to devise a route that incorporates three specific goals before reaching the final destination. The task was to be resolved in groups, and children were not allowed to point to the map. This last instruction was given to elicit as much vocabulary from the children as possible.

3.3 Data Collection and Analysis

On the day of the activity, audio recorders were placed on the students' tables. Additionally, each teacher was given a personal recorder with a microphone.

Every audio recording underwent transcription and subsequent anonymisation. A unique code was assigned to each student and teacher, which was then employed both in the transcriptions and for linking to their demographic information and test scores. The coding and analysis process was facilitated through NVivo, a software utilised not only for coding transcriptions but also for quantifying the occurrences of relevant codes central to the study. The codes analysed for current purposes were:

- Addressing a girl
  - Giving a turn to a girl
  - Giving feedback to a girl
    - Enforcing following instructions
    - Correcting navigation production
    - Positive

- Addressing a boy
  - Giving a turn to a boy
  - Giving feedback to a boy
    - Enforcing following instructions
    - Correcting navigation production
    - Positive

- Voluntary participation in class by gender

SPSS software was utilised for both descriptive statistics and statistical data analysis. To assess gender in teacher-student interactions, the aggregate count of teachers addressing individual students was tallied for each class. Subsequently, this total was utilised to calculate the percentage of interactions directed towards girls and boys, respectively. An independent t-test was then conducted to ascertain the statistical significance of any observed differences in the percentages of interactions targeting boys or girls. A parallel procedure was applied to analyse students' participation percentages. Conversely, for nominal variables such as the types of feedback offered, a chi-square test was employed to examine potential associations between type of feedback and gender. Concerning students' performance, the averages of groups initiating and completing the route in each class were computed, and these values were aggregated to determine the overall percentages for the year. A parallel procedure was employed for assessing the time taken to finish the route. The gender-specific analysis involved noting which student took the lead in mixed-gender groups, and the resulting percentages were categorised by gender.

4 Results

4.1 Interaction with Students

In the three classes of Year 5, teachers exhibited a more hands-on approach to their students' activity progress than teachers in Year 6. Notably, while interactions with boys remained relatively consistent, interactions with girls significantly decreased. This is shown in Fig. 1 (error bars show standard error).

In general, teachers from Year 6 addressed their students significantly less than teachers from Year 5, $F(1,4) = 9.689, p = .036$. While Fig. 1 delineates the cumulative raw instances of teachers' interactions, Fig. 2 provides a percentage representation by amalgamating outcomes across all classes in each year.

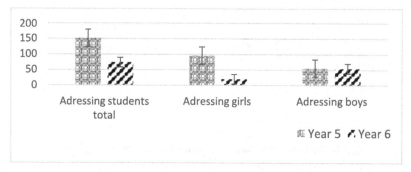

Fig. 1. Teachers addressing students in general and by gender (number of instances).

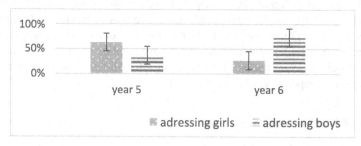

Fig. 2. Percentage of teachers addressing students by gender

To address variation in student numbers, a data set was created that showed how many times each student was addressed and a 2x2 ANOVA test was executed. The outcomes revealed a significant interaction effect between gender and year ($f(1,108) = 8.296$, $p = .005$). Further scrutiny through pairwise comparisons indicated that the number of comments directed towards girls was significantly lower in Year 6 compared to girls in Year 5. The results also yielded noteworthy gender disparities in both academic years, with a statistical trend toward favouring girls in Year 5 ($t(46) = 1.988$, $p = .053$) and a significant proclivity towards boys in Year 6 ($t(62) = -2.035$, $p = .046$).

4.2 Students' Voluntary Participation

Voluntary participation in this context refers to instances where students either raised their hand and were subsequently invited by the teacher to contribute or spontaneously offered input relevant to the class topic without explicit prompting.

Throughout the task, it was observed that teachers conscientiously endeavoured to alternate between genders when soliciting participation. Nevertheless, despite this deliberate attempt to uphold gender equality in participation, an observable incongruity persists in the level of participation based on gender. Figure 3 illustrates the mean percentage of student participation categorised by gender.

In Year 6, a discernible change is observed in students' voluntary participation, marked by a decline in girls' involvement and an increase in boys' engagement, leading to an expanded overall participation gap. It's important to note that this difference,

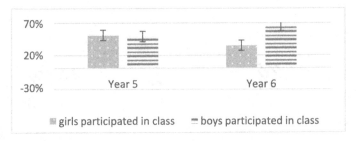

Fig. 3. Students' percentage of voluntary participation by gender

though notable, does not reach statistical significance. Nevertheless, while Year 5 does not present a gender difference in participation, Year 6 does (t (4) = 3.546, p = .024). More than the students' gender might be playing a role in this observation. One plausible hypothesis is that the preferential attention from the teacher towards a particular gender could be impacting students' confidence levels in voluntary participation. To explore this further, a closer examination of the types of interactions teachers have with their students becomes imperative.

4.3 Type of Teacher-Student Interaction

A noteworthy shift is observed from girls receiving more engagement from the teacher than boys in Year 5 to the opposite trend in Year 6 (Fig. 4). However, statistical analysis revealed that the sole significant difference between Year 5 and Year 6 pertains to the "giving feedback to girls" category: $t(4) = 3.101$, $p = .036$, signifying that teachers in Year 6 provided less feedback to girls compared to Year 5.

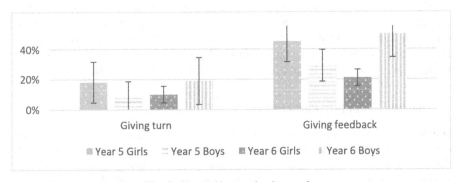

Fig. 4. Type of interaction by gender

A thorough examination of the feedback provided to students (Fig. 5) was conducted to investigate the observed gender difference. A chi-square test revealed a significant association between gender and the type of feedback teachers generally imparted: X^2 (2, N = 163) = 21.974, $p = .000$. This means that the type of feedback a student received seems to be associated with their gender. This association persisted when examining each year separately—Year 5: X^2 (2, N = 112) = 9.254, p = .010, and Year 6: X^2 (2, N = 51) = 13.756, p = .001.

Upon establishing the significant relationship between gender and feedback type in both years, the Phi value was computed to quantify the strength of this relationship. The Phi value was found to be .287 in Year 5, indicating a weak relationship, whereas it increased to .519 in Year 6, signifying a strong relationship [1].

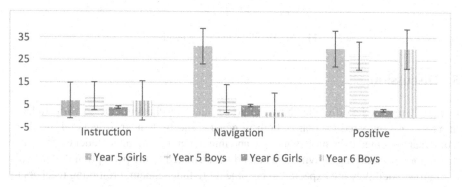

Fig. 5. Type of feedback by gender

In Year 6, teachers not only demonstrated a higher frequency of feedback given to boys compared to girls $(X^2$ (2, N = 51) = 13.756, p = .001) but also exhibited a significant imbalance in positive feedback, with boys receiving considerably more positive feedback than girls. Additionally, in both years, teachers provided less corrective feedback to boys for navigation than would be anticipated in the absence of any gender-related association, surpassing the expected feedback for girls. A similar pattern is observed in positive feedback, where boys receive more commendations than anticipated, while girls receive less than expected if there was no relation to gender. Regarding following instructions, corrections for boys, both for following and not following instructions, are more prevalent in both years compared to corrections for girls.

4.4 Students' Performance

When comparing the aggregate performance of classes from each academic year, students seemed to perform better in Year 5. In Year 5, 95% initiated and 81.25% successfully completed the route, whereas in Year 6, 75% initiated and 62.5% successfully completed the route. Average completion time in Year 5 was 5:16 minutes, and 6:23 in Year 6. However, these differences were not statistically significant. Instead, a significant gender difference was found concerning activity leadership, with boys taking the lead more frequently in Year 6 compared to Year 5 $(t(4) = -5.333, p = .006)$ (Fig. 6).

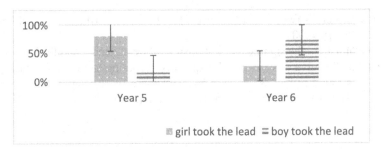

Fig. 6. Activity's leader by gender

5 Discussion

Our study revealed a difference between how science teachers interacted with students in Year 5 as compared to Year 6, both in general and by gender. In general, teachers from Year 5 seemed to be more hands-on and interact more with their students, engaging them more often during activity. This could be attributed to the perception that as children grow older, they are expected to become more independent, prompting teachers to reduce their interaction during activity time. However, the observed divergence in how teachers address children based on gender is more intricately nuanced and warrants a more comprehensive explanation.

There are two possible explanations for the observed gendered shift in teachers' behaviour between the two years. First, children at this age might be displaying emerging gender differences in spatial ability [12, 34], influencing their performance in class. Teachers could subconsciously recognise this and engage more with the group exhibiting higher proficiency. However, in our study, there was no significant gender difference in spatial ability in Year 6, and no significant difference was observed between the two years.

Secondly, consistent with findings from prior research (e.g., [5, 11]), gender as a factor influencing teachers' interactions with children may surface more clearly at this key age range. Despite teachers not explicitly mentioning gender in their responses regarding students who would excel or encounter difficulties with the task, their interactions reveal the presence of unconscious gender stereotypes. Although it was observed that teachers consciously aimed for gender-balanced participation by alternating between genders, a discernible preference for boys emerged when addressing groups separately or interacting with students who volunteered without prompting. In other words, this bias seems to be particularly pronounced in their monitoring interactions rather than in collective engagement. Moreover, this bias appears to be unconsciously internalised, which is why it seems to be influencing their behaviour despite their explicit efforts to achieve gender-balanced participation and avoid using gender-specific terms when addressing the entire class. These findings align with observations from Whyte's [40] study, where biases favouring boys were likewise unconscious, with teachers mistakenly perceiving their attention allocation as balanced when, in reality, it leaned toward boys.

The correlation between teachers' engagement and students' voluntary participation unveils notable gender dynamics. When teachers engage more with girls than with boys, girls' participation closely resembles that of boys, while increased engagement with boys widens the participation gap in favour of boys. This finding echoes Flores' [11] observations in mathematics education, where teachers' preferential engagement with male students affected girls' willingness to participate. Moreover, given the negligible difference in ability between genders, children's gender identity development and teachers' level of engagement likely have a greater impact on voluntary participation than children's confidence in their abilities.

This observation gains significance within the context of the recorded science class activity involving a navigation task. Past research, such as studies by Neuburger et al. [22, 23] and Nguyen & Ryan [26], underscores the potential for stereotype threat in such educational settings, particularly affecting girls' performance and participation. Consequently, if girls internalise stereotypes suggesting their inferiority in science and navigation, they may experience reduced confidence, leading to a diminished inclination to volunteer in class. This phenomenon unfolds along a sequential chain: the prevailing belief that "boys are better at maths and science" is widely recognized [3]. Additionally, around this age, children become increasingly aware of their gender identity [28], resulting in a heightened internalisation of gender stereotypes [18]. Collectively, these factors contribute to a diminished sense of confidence and performance in the particular context of this science class.

Another noteworthy aspect is the impact of feedback. The observed higher instances of correcting behaviour and offering positive feedback to boys compared to girls, as well as correcting girls' navigation more often aligns with prior gender-related classroom studies (e.g., [11, 13]). However, there is an interesting observation when looking at this in relation to voluntary participation. In Year 5, despite girls receiving more frequent navigation corrections than boys and a higher ratio of corrections to positive feedback, their participation levels remained comparable to boys'. In contrast, the decline in girls' voluntary participation in Year 6 coincides with a notable decrease in positive feedback provided to girls. This suggests that positive feedback could significantly influence students' confidence and comfort levels in participating. The reasons for this decrease in positive feedback can only be speculated based on previous studies. For instance, van den Brink and Stobes [38] found that despite higher involvement and better performance, female science students may be perceived by faculty as less suitable for careers in science, indicating a common internalised gender bias where girls' and women's performance is viewed as inferior to that of men. This bias seems to be reflected in increased praise for boys in classroom situations and a distorted perception of suitability for female science students.

Factors such as heightened engagement and increased positive feedback directed towards boys can strongly affect girls' comfort levels in expressing themselves, both in class and in mixed-gender groups. Despite no difference in spatial ability, there is a noticeable decline in girls' leadership roles in group tasks in Year 6 compared to Year 5. This suggests that participants in mixed groups may not be assuming leadership based on their actual abilities but rather on their perceived abilities, with girls exhibiting lower confidence than boys. This aligns with studies demonstrating that at this age, girls' confidence in their spatial ability tends to decrease [21, 34]. The idea that teachers might be reinforcing this belief through their actions is also consistent with previous studies (e.g., [11, 13]).

In all the aspects discussed, gender appears to exert a notable influence on children's and teachers' behaviours. Children who have internalised gender stereotypes may demonstrate distinct tendencies, such as boys being more inclined to vocalise contributions, interrupt, and volunteer, while girls might exhibit a reluctance to express their answers in a mixed, collective setting. On the teachers' side, their responses might be influenced unconsciously by these gendered behaviours, potentially reinforcing them by engaging and praising boys more, especially in the older year.

The intricate interplay observed between children and teachers might potentially exert a profound impact on children's academic performance and attitudes towards STEM subjects. This observation resonates with existing literature indicating that during this developmental stage, significant gender differences in spatial ability, a crucial factor for STEM performance, begin to manifest [12, 34]. While acknowledging the role of developmental factors, the significance of the learning environment should not be underestimated.

Many interventions aimed at mitigating the gender gap in STEM predominantly concentrate on the "supply side," emphasising the development of spatial ability. However, it is imperative for research to equally address the "demand side", particularly during the critical timeframe when gender differences begin to widen. Given the substantiated influence of stereotype threat in task performance [20, 31] and ability development [16, 22], there is a pressing need for a deliberate effort to minimise its impact, especially during the formative years. This case study, albeit limited in scope, is particularly compelling as it reveals that, despite the school's strong emphasis on science and teachers' clear efforts toward gender equity, gender biases are still discernibly influencing classroom dynamics. Ongoing research aims to investigate further if these biases also extend to impact the task performance of the children involved.

6   Conclusions

This case study exemplifies the potential impact of internalised gender stereotypes on classroom interactions, even in instances where teachers consciously strive for gender equity. Preferential attention towards boys might influence girls' willingness to participate in class actively and their self-concept of ability. Positive reinforcement appears more influential than corrective measures in encouraging student engagement. These insights are crucial for addressing gender disparities in spatial abilities, especially in intervention development. Prior research has already emphasised the role of various activities in spatial ability development (e.g., [22]). Future research endeavours could delve deeper into exploring the longitudinal effects of gender biases on classroom dynamics and academic outcomes, considering the critical age range where these biases may surface more prominently. Additionally, investigating the efficacy of interventions aimed at mitigating gender disparities in STEM fields, particularly during formative years, warrants attention. Moreover, this study contributes to the broader discourse on early childhood education by highlighting the pervasive influence of gender stereotypes on children's confidence and participation in STEM-related activities. By elucidating the complex dynamics of teacher and child interactions and their impact on class engagement, this research extends previous studies and underscores the need for comprehensive interventions to promote gender equity in education.

Acknowledgements. This study was part of the SellSTEM project and funded by the European Union's Horizon 2020 programme under the Marie Skłodowska-Curie grant agreement 956124.

Disclosure of Interests. The authors have no competing interests to declare that are relevant to the content of this article.

References

1. Akoglu, H.: User's guide to correlation coefficients. Turkish J. Emerg. Med. **18**(3), 91–93 (2018). https://doi.org/10.1016/j.tjem.2018.08.001
2. Bartlett, K.A., Camba, J.D.: Gender differences in spatial ability: a critical review. Educ. Psychol. Rev. **35**(1) Article 8. Springer (2023). https://doi.org/10.1007/s10648-023-09728-2
3. Bigler, R.S., Liben, L.S.: Developmental intergroup theory explaining and reducing children's social stereotyping and prejudice. Curr. Dir. Psychol. Sci. **16**(3), 162–166 (2006)
4. Chen, E.S.L., Rao, N.: Gender socialisation in Chinese kindergartens: teachers' contributions. Sex Roles **64**(1), 103–116 (2011). https://doi.org/10.1007/s11199-010-9873-4
5. Coates, J.: Women, men, and language. In: Leech, G., Short, M., (Eds.) 3rd ed. Pearson Education Limited (2004)
6. Collaer, M.L., Hines, M.: No evidence for enhancement of spatial ability with elevated prenatal androgen exposure in congenital adrenal hyperplasia: a meta-analysis. Arch. Sex. Behav. **49**(2), 395–411 (2020). https://doi.org/10.1007/s10508-020-01645-7
7. Connel, R.: Gender in world perspective. Polity Press (2021)
8. Crawford, M.: Talking difference: on gender and language. SAGE Publications, Limited (1995)
9. Deutschmann, M., Steinvall, A., Lindvall-Östling, M.: Raising awareness about gender and language among teacher-training students: a cross-cultural approach. Open Linguist. **7**(1), 666–684 (2021). https://doi.org/10.1515/opli-2020-0181
10. Espinosa, G.: Currículo y equidad de género en la primaria: una mirada desde el aula: estudio realizado en tres escuelas estatales de la ciudad Lima.[Curriculum and gender equality in primary: a look from the classroom] In Educacion y procesos pedagogicos y equidad: cuatro informes de investigacion, pp. 69–129 (2004)
11. Flores, R.: Representaciones de genero en el desempeno matematico de estudiantes de secundaria. [Gender representations in secondary students' math performance]. Revista Iberoamericana de Educacion, **43**, 103–118 (2007)
12. Frick, A., Möhring, W., Newcombe, N.S.: Development of mental transformation abilities. Trends Cogn. Sci. **18**(10), 536–542 (2014). https://doi.org/10.1016/j.tics.2014.05.011
13. Gamboa Araya, R.: ¿Equidad de género en la enseñanza de las Matemáticas? [Gender equality in math teaching?] Revista Electrónica Educare **16**(1), 63–78 (2012). https://doi.org/10.15359/ree.16-1.6
14. Halpern, D.F.: Sex differences in cognitive abilitied, 3rd edn. Erlbaum (2000)
15. Hughes, C.C., Schilt, K., Gorman, B.K., Bratter, J.L.: Framing the faculty gender gap: a view from STEM doctoral students. Gend. Work. Organ. **24**(4), 398–416 (2017). https://doi.org/10.1111/gwao.12174

16. Liben, L.S., Bigler, R.S.: The developmental course of gender differentiation: conceptualizing, measuring, and evaluating constructs and pathways. Monographs Soc. Res. Child Develop. **67**, 1–183 (2002). https://doi.org/10.1111/1540-5834.00189

17. Linn, M.C., Petersen, A.C.: Emergence and characterisation of sex differences in spatial ability: a meta-analysis. Child Dev. **56**(6), 1479–1498 (1985)

18. Mckown, C., Weinstein, R.: The development and consequences of stereotype consciousness in middle-childhood. Child Dev. **74**, 498–515 (2003)

19. Moè, A.: Gender difference does not mean genetic difference: externalizing improves performance in mental rotation. Learn. Individ. Differ. **22**(1), 20–24 (2012). https://doi.org/10.1016/j.lindif.2011.11.001

20. Moè, A., Pazzaglia, F.: Following the instructions! Effects of gender beliefs in mental rotation. Learn. Individ. Differ. **16**(4), 369–377 (2006). https://doi.org/10.1016/j.lindif.2007.01.002

21. Neuburger, S., Jansen, P., Heil, M., Quaiser-Pohl, C.: Gender differences in pre-adolescents' mental-rotation performance: do they depend on grade and stimulus type? Personality Individ. Differ. **50**(8), 1238–1242 (2011). https://doi.org/10.1016/j.paid.2011.02.017

22. Neuburger, S., Jansen, P., Heil, M., Quaiser-Pohl, C.: A threat in the classroom: gender stereotype activation and mental-rotation performance in elementary-school children. Zeitschrift Fur Psychologie/J. Psychol. **220**(2), 61–69 (2012). https://doi.org/10.1027/2151-2604/a000097

23. Neuburger, S., Ruthsatz, V., Jansen, P., Quaiser-Pohl, C.: Can girls think spatially? Influence of implicit gender stereotype activation and rotational axis on fourth graders' mental-rotation performance. Learn. Individ. Differ. **37**, 169–175 (2015). https://doi.org/10.1016/j.lindif.2014.09.003

24. Newcombe, N., Bandura, M.M., Taylor, D.G.: Sex differences in spatial ability and spatial activities. Sex Roles **9**(3), 377–386 (1983)

25. Newcombe, N.S.: The puzzle of spatial sex differences: current status and prerequisites to solutions. Child Develop. Perspect. **14**(4), 251–257 (2020). https://doi.org/10.1111/cdep.12389

26. Nguyen, H.D., Ryan, A.M.: Does stereotype threat affect test performance of minorities and women. J. Appl. Psychol. **93**, 1314–1334 (2008)

27. Ramful, A., Lowrie, T., Logan, T.: Measurement of spatial ability: construction and validation of the spatial reasoning instrument for middle school students. J. Psychoeduc. Assess. **35**(7), 709–727 (2017)

28. Ruble, D.N., Martin, C.L.: Gender development. In: Eisenberg, N., (ed.) Handbook of Child Psychology: Social, Emotional and Personality Development, 5th edn, vol. 3, pp. 993–1016. Wiley, NY (1998)

29. Sadker, M., Sadker, D.: Sexism in the schoolroom of the 80's. Psychol. Today 54–57 (1985)

30. Spender, D.: Invisible women: the schooling scandal. Women's Press (1990)

31. Steele, C.M.: A threat in the air. Am. Psychol. **52**, 613–629 (1997)

32. Sunderland, J.: New understanding of gender and language classroom research: Texts, teacher talk and student talk. Lang. Teach. Res. **4**(2), 149–173 (2000). https://doi.org/10.1177/136216880000400204

33. Tan, E., Calabrese Barton, A., Kang, H., O'Neil, T.: Desiring a career in STEM-related fields: How middle school girls articulate and negotiate identities- inpractice in science. J. Res. Sci. Teach. **50**(10), 1143–1179 (2013)

34. Titze, C., Jansen, P., Heil, M.: Mental rotation performance and the effect of gender in fourth graders and adults. Eur. J. Develop. Psychol. **7**(4), 432–444 (2010). https://doi.org/10.1080/17405620802548214

35. Tzuriel, D., Egozi, G.: Gender differences in spatial ability of young children: The effects of training and processing strategies. Child Dev. **81**(5), 1417–1430 (2010)

36. Uttal, D.H., Cohen, C.A.: Spatial Thinking and STEM Education: when, Why, and How? Psychol. Learn. Motiv. Adv. Res. Theory **57**, 147–181 (2012). https://doi.org/10.1016/B978-0-12-394293-7.00004-2
37. Uttal, D.H., et al.: The malleability of spatial skills: a meta-analysis of training studies. Psychol. Bull. **139**(2), 352–402 (2013). https://doi.org/10.1037/A0028446
38. van den Brink, M., Stobbe, L.: Doing gender in academic education: the paradox of visibility. Gend. Work. Organ. **16**(4), 451–470 (2009)
39. Verdine, B.N., Golinkoff, R.M., Hirsh-Pasek, K., Newcombe, N.S.: Finding the missing piece: blocks, puzzles, and shapes fuel school readiness. Trends Neurosci. Educ. **3**(1), 7–13 (2014). https://doi.org/10.1016/j.tine.2014.02.005
40. Whyte, J.: Getting the GIST. Routledge & Kegan Paul (1986)
41. Xu, Y., Martin, C.: Gender differences in STEM disciplines: from the aspects of informal professional networking and faculty career development. Gend. Issues **28**(3), 134–154 (2011)

Cognitive Perspectives on Perceived Spatial Ability in STEM

Meryn McNea[1]([✉]) [iD], Reena Cole[1] [iD], David Tanner[1] [iD], and Diarmaid Lane[2] [iD]

[1] School of Engineering, University of Limerick, Limerick, Ireland
`meryn.mcnea@ul.ie`
[2] School of Education, University of Limerick, Limerick, Ireland

Abstract. Spatial ability, crucial for success in science, technology, engineering, and mathematics (STEM) fields, displays intriguing gender differences, particularly in tasks involving spatial visualisation and mental rotation. This paper explores the nuanced landscape of gender-related cognitive processing disparities in spatial tasks, contributing to a broader understanding of cognitive diversity. While males tend to outperform females in spatial visualisation and mental rotation tasks, the impact of timing on these assessments reveals a more multifaceted picture, emphasising the importance of considering testing conditions and methodologies. The focus on mental rotation tasks extends beyond research to practical applications in education and vocational settings. Gender disparities in performance, especially under time constraints, prompt an exploration of motivational factors and societal influences. Cognitive differences in mental rotation tasks between genders involve distinct processing approaches. Typically, females exhibit top-down processing, whereas males adopt a bottom-up approach. Significant individual variations within each gender highlight the influence of diverse factors, including biology, environment, and culture on cognitive processes. This cognitive dichotomy provides insights into the varied strategies individuals employ in spatial tasks, emphasising the complexity and diversity of cognitive processes. The paper emphasises the need for inclusive and context-aware approaches when interpreting gender differences in spatial cognition, offering a nuanced perspective on cognitive diversity. Engaging with this research will equip readers with a deeper understanding of the complex interplay between biological, environmental, and cultural factors, ultimately contributing to a more informed and inclusive approach to the study of spatial cognition.

Keywords: Spatial Ability · Spatial Cognition · Cognitive Processing · Mental Rotation · Top-Down Processing · Bottom-Up Processing

1 Introduction

Spatial ability, the aptitude to perceive, understand, and manipulate spatial relationships among objects, plays a pivotal role in various cognitive tasks, particularly those integral to science, technology, engineering, and mathematics (STEM) fields. Proficiency

M. Živković et al. (Eds.): Spatial Cognition 2024, LNAI 14756, pp. 66–78, 2024.
https://doi.org/10.1007/978-3-031-63115-3_5

in spatial thinking is crucial for tasks such as problem-solving, navigation, and understanding complex visual information [1]. As STEM disciplines continue to advance, the significance of spatial ability becomes increasingly apparent, influencing academic and professional success [2, 3]. However, within the realm of spatial cognition, intriguing patterns emerge, with research suggesting notable gender differences in how individuals approach and solve spatial problems. This paper delves into the complexities of gender-related cognitive processing disparities when engaging with spatial visualisation tests, specifically mental rotation, contributing to a deeper understanding of cognitive diversity on a broader scale. To this end, this paper addresses two central research questions.

(1) What are the gender-related differences in key cognitive processes associated with spatial cognition, and how do neurobiological variations contribute to these differences?
(2) In what ways can research findings inform the design of inclusive educational strategies and interventions to accommodate diverse gender-related spatial cognitive patterns?

The research methodology employed in this study consisted of conducting a narrative review. The process of topic selection began with the identification of pivotal themes such as "cognitive processing," "cognitive diversity," "mental rotation test," and "problem solving." These themes were systematically explored through searches conducted on Google Scholar, with a preference for selecting journal articles presented empirical data and theoretical frameworks grounded in cognitive psychology and spatial research. Additionally, studies focusing on gender differences in spatial cognition, particularly those employing standardised spatial ability assessments such as the Mental Rotation Test (MRT), were prioritised. To ensure inclusion of emerging seminal research, a multifaceted methodology was employed that included regularly monitoring preprint servers, setting up alerts for relevant keywords across diverse academic databases, and actively engaging with interdisciplinary journals.

Subsequently, a literature review was conducted. This phase involved the extraction and analysis of relevant data from the identified articles, thus providing a comprehensive overview of existing research in the field. By employing this methodology, the paper aims to provide a thorough exploration of gender-related cognitive processing disparities in spatial cognition, offering valuable insights for both academic research and practical applications in educational settings.

Spatial ability, a multifaceted cognitive skill, encompasses various components such as spatial visualisation, spatial perception, and spatial memory [1]. These components collectively contribute to an individual's capacity to comprehend and manipulate spatial relationships among objects. Extensive research has been conducted to explore potential gender differences in spatial ability, shedding light on the intricacies of cognitive processing. One prominent area of investigation revolves around spatial visualisation, which involves mentally manipulating and transforming two and/or three-dimensional shapes. Studies suggest that, on average, males tend to outperform females in tasks requiring spatial visualization [4–6]. This difference has been attributed to various factors, including both biological and environmental influences. Some researchers propose that hormonal differences during brain development may contribute to variations in spatial cognitive abilities between genders [7, 8]. Additionally, societal expectations and experiences, such as differences in childhood play patterns or exposure to spatially demanding activities, may also play a role [9–11]. Another facet of spatial ability is mental rotation, which involves mentally rotating objects in one's mind. Research indicates that males often exhibit an enhanced ability in mental rotation tasks compared to females [12–15]. This discrepancy has been observed across various age groups, suggesting that it may not solely be a result of developmental factors but could have roots in fundamental cognitive processes. However, it is crucial to note that these observed differences are general trends, and considerable variability exists within each gender group.

Interestingly, when the timed element is removed from mental rotation tests, the observed sex differences in performance tend to reduce [14, 16]. In many studies, the time constraint appears to introduce an additional layer of complexity that disproportionately affects females. Without the pressure of time, both males and females exhibit more comparable levels of proficiency in mental rotation tasks. This finding suggests that the gender disparities observed in timed assessments might be influenced by factors beyond the inherent cognitive abilities, such as test-taking strategies, anxiety, or the speed-accuracy trade-off [17–20].

Sheryl Sorby's spatial intervention provides further insights into addressing these gender-related cognitive differences. Sorby (2009) emphasises the role of spatial visualisation training, particularly among engineering students, to enhance spatial abilities. Her approach employs structured exercises targeting mental rotation and spatial visualisation skills, aiming to narrow the gender gap evident in these areas [21]. By integrating this direct intervention, researchers can gain valuable insights into the nuanced factors influencing gender disparities in spatial cognition. This underscores the importance of considering testing conditions and methodologies in interpreting and generalising findings within spatial cognition research, emphasising the necessity for inclusive and context-aware approaches in studying gender differences in cognitive processing.

2   Mental Rotation Tasks

The mental rotation test (MRT) is a cognitive assessment tool that measures an individual's spatial visualisation ability. This evaluative instrument, developed by psychologists Vandenberg and Kuse in 1978 [22], seeks to quantify the capacity for mental rotation, encompassing two-dimensional projections of three-dimensional objects, thereby unveiling the intricacies of spatial reasoning skills. Participants engage in a cognitive challenge, tasked with determining whether a series of paired images are identical or mirror images after mentally rotating one of them (Fig. 1).

The mental rotation test has a wide range of applications outside of research. It is a valuable asset in the field of psychological and cognitive science research for investigating spatial abilities [14, 23–25]. Its use allows for a comprehensive investigation of the interactions between spatial reasoning skills and other cognitive functions, resulting in a more comprehensive understanding of cognitive processes. Beyond research, the test has practical applications in educational and vocational settings. Mental rotation tests are employed across a range of fields, including mathematics, engineering, and architecture [26]. This evaluative tool measures a person's spatial reasoning abilities by testing their ability to mentally manipulate both two- and three-dimensional objects. The

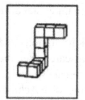 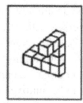 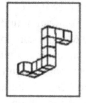

Fig. 1. Each Mental Rotation Test item consists of a row of 5-line drawings, including a target figure in the left position followed by 4 choice figures. The task is to indicate which of the 4 response choice figures are rotated reproductions of the left figure [22].

mental rotation test is especially useful for professions that require strong spatial skills, as it provides insights that go beyond the theoretical realm. The results provide useful information about an individual's cognitive profile, which can influence educational and career decisions. Based on these findings, educational institutions can tailor instructional strategies, and employers can make informed decisions about job placements that match an individual's cognitive strengths. Consequently, this facilitates a more judicious and informed decision-making process in the realm of career placements [27].

The Mental Rotation Test despite its popularity and contributions to theoretical advances in cognitive science, faces critical limitations that question its reliability and validity in assessing mental rotation ability. Shepard and Metzler's [4] initial experiments demonstrated a linear relationship between rotation degree and response time, suggesting a direct link to mental rotation processes. However, subsequent research challenges this view, with Caissie et al. 2009 [23] proposing that factors beyond mental rotation, such as figure perception and comparison, contribute significantly to item difficulty on the MRT. Bors and Vigneau [28] further highlight gender differences in MRT performance unrelated to the ability to mentally rotate objects, indicating the presence of alternative cognitive processes.

Stimulus construction adds another layer of complexity, as the MRT deviates from Shepard and Metzler's preference for perspective drawings, using parallel projection drawings instead. This choice introduces distortions and ambiguity in the stimuli, impacting the test-taker's ability to accurately interpret and mentally rotate shapes. The inclusion of occluded parts in the revised MRT further complicates matters, requiring test-takers to rely on strategies beyond mental rotation, undermining the test's specificity [15]. Moreover, issues of test reliability emerge, as even one repeat test leads to significant performance improvement, suggesting potential practice effects and questioning the stability of the measure over time.

In light of these concerns, the broader applications of the MRT in bridging theoretical cognitive research with real-world implications must be critically examined. While the MRT has been influential in cognitive science, its practical utility in educational and vocational settings may be compromised by the identified limitations. To address these shortcomings, researchers advocate for a revised MRT [29] that aligns more closely with Shepard and Metzler's original methodology, incorporating perspective drawings and eliminating occluded parts. Such improvements could enhance the accuracy and reliability of the MRT, ensuring that it continues to be a valuable tool in understanding mental rotation processes and their application in diverse contexts.

In summary, the critique of the Mental Rotation Test highlights its limitations and prompts the need for a revised version that better aligns with cognitive research. Yet, the complexities of gender differences in spatial cognition demand a comprehensive understanding of the interplay between biological, cultural, and cognitive factors [30]. Achieving this refined perspective is crucial for refining assessment tools and interventions, bridging the gap between.

2.1 Gender Performance

As previously mentioned, studies have consistently highlighted that, on average, males tend to outperform females in tasks with a timed element [2, 14, 15]. However, recent research [31] highlights that when the time constraint is removed – the gender differences become less noticeable. In scenarios where individuals have ample time to navigate mental rotation problems without the pressure of time constraints, the previously observed gender gap tends to diminish. This phenomenon prompts a deeper examination of the role of speed in assessing cognitive abilities and its potential contribution to the apparent disparities between genders.

Some researchers suggest that the imposition of time constraints in various tests could disadvantage females, as they might prioritise accuracy over speed [32]. Removing the time constraint allows individuals to rely more on their intrinsic spatial reasoning abilities rather than feeling compelled to respond swiftly, providing a more accurate representation of their underlying cognitive skills. Moreover, delving into socio-cultural factors [15] is crucial in understanding the observed gender differences. Stereotypes and societal expectations can significantly influence individuals' confidence levels and their approach to spatial tasks [33]. Eliminating the time limit allows individuals to approach mental rotation problems at their own pace, potentially mitigating the impact of external influences such as stereotypes. As researchers explore the complex interplay of timing, spatial abilities, and societal expectations, it becomes increasingly evident that considering various factors is essential for interpreting and understanding gender-related disparities in mental rotation problem-solving.

The elucidation of gender disparities in spatial abilities encompasses diverse perspectives, with one perspective attributing these distinctions to biological factors. Spatial tasks are closely associated with the right parietal regions of the brain, and males often exhibit heightened specialisation in the right hemisphere, while females tend to utilise the left hemisphere for both verbal and non-verbal tasks [34, 35].

The prenatal exposure of the fetus to varying hormonal levels based on gender is posited to influence brain development, offering a biological explanation reinforced by the observed male superiority in mental rotation tasks. However, cultural influences [34] are recognised as significant contributors to gender differences in spatial abilities. The perception of spatial ability as predominantly masculine may shape self-perceptions and performance outcomes. Males, influenced by cultural stereotypes, perceive themselves as adept in spatial tasks, actively engaging in and excelling at them. Conversely, females may perceive themselves as less proficient and interested, potentially influenced by prevailing cultural norms [33]. Consequently, this cultural bias may lead to divergent engagement levels in spatial tasks, influencing choices in toys and educational paths that emphasise spatial abilities, ultimately fostering greater expertise in this domain among males.

Motivational factors [19, 36] also play a role in explaining gender differences in mental rotation tests. Females tend to approach these tests with greater caution, investing more time in the process, whereas males exhibit quicker decision-making when selecting items corresponding to a specific target. It has been observed that given sufficient time or when manipulating participants' expectations, females can perform nearly as accurately as their male counterparts [14]. This underscores the importance of considering motivational aspects in understanding and interpreting gender differences in spatial abilities.

Although Voyer [37] initially attributed the reduction in gender differences in the 40-point scoring scheme to women guessing more frequently than men, their subsequent study in 2004 revealed a different perspective. According to their later findings, men exhibited a higher overall tendency to guess on the Mental Rotation Test compared to women [38]. The focal point of discussions on gender disparities in mental rotation tasks has been the role of time constraints, with studies indicating that eliminating such pressures diminishes the apparent gender gap. The research by Voyer [37, 38] contributes to this discourse by emphasising the convoluted relationship between guessing behaviour and gender differences. While recognising the potential influence of biological factors on spatial abilities, it is crucial not to overlook the impact of cultural influences and motivational aspects. The removal of time limits allows individuals to demonstrate their intrinsic spatial reasoning abilities without being constrained by societal expectations and stereotypes [15]. Navigating the complex landscape of gender-related disparities in mental rotation problem-solving requires a consideration of various factors to ensure a comprehensive and unbiased understanding of cognitive differences between genders.

3 Male Versus Female Brain

The human brain's adaptability complicates our understanding of cognitive disparities between genders, challenging the idea of a linear distinction. The observed differences in engagement during mental rotation tasks may stem from adaptive strategies in specific contexts rather than fixed characteristics [39]. Cognitive functionality extends beyond rigid gender-based patterns, with the brain exhibiting dynamic and adaptable processes. As individuals navigate tasks, the brain's ability to reconfigure networks challenges static interpretations of cognitive disparities, highlighting the importance of considering a spectrum of approaches instead of a binary view based on gender. Additionally, the intricacies of top-down and bottom-up cognitive processing in problem-solving, adds complexity [40]. These approaches may not be exclusive to a particular gender but reflect individual variations influenced by factors such as experience, learning, and environmental cues. The non-linear nature of cognitive processing challenges stereotypes, emphasising the need for an integrative approach when exploring the interplay between gender and cognition.

Top-down processing, also referred to as concept or theory-driven processing, represents a cognitive mechanism wherein incoming sensory information is construed utilising pre-existing knowledge, expectations, and contextual cues [41]. By starting with general impressions and working down to specific details, top-down information processing enables us to interpret information that has already been gathered by the senses. In contrast to bottom-up processing, which initiates analysis based on individual stimulus features, top-down processing originates from higher-level cognitive processes and expectations [42]. This cognitive phenomenon occurs when the brain interprets and comprehends incoming sensory information based on prior knowledge, experiential insights, and expectations. For example, when confronted with a blurred image of a person's face, top-down processing facilitates the brain's utilisation of prior knowledge of facial features to extrapolate missing details [43], aiding in the recognition of the individual. Top-down processing is subject to various influencing factors such as attention, motivation, and contextual considerations. Its functionality enables rapid comprehension of complex stimuli and situations by leveraging past experiences and accumulated knowledge (Fig. 2).

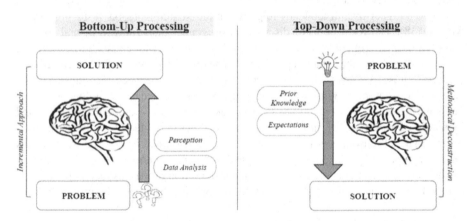

Fig. 2. Bottom-Up versus Top-Down Processing in Problem Solving.

Bottom-up processing is a cognitive processing approach in which information is received and interpreted based on the incoming sensory data without relying heavily on pre-existing knowledge or expectations. This type of processing involves the analysis of individual components or features of the stimulus, and the integration of these components to form a complete perception [24]. In short, information travels "up" from stimuli through the senses to the brain, where it is passively translated in the bottom-up process. Illustrating this concept with a practical example, consider a situation where an individual recently experiences the discomfort of stubbing their toe against the corner of a bed. Following this incident, the pain receptors in the toe promptly detect the sensation of pain and transmit corresponding signals to the brain, thereby instigating the processing of this pain sensation. In this context, the cognitive process aligns with bottom-up processing, as the brain directly receives signals of pain from the sensory receptors in the toe, devoid of substantial reliance on prior knowledge or expectations. Conversely, subsequent to this painful event, the individual's heightened awareness [40] triggers a deliberate exercise of caution around the bed's corners. This enhanced vigilance arises from the recollection of the intense pain linked to the prior toe-stubbing incident, presenting an exemplification of top-down processing. In this scenario, the individual's preceding knowledge and memory of the distressing experience actively influence their behaviour, as they conscientiously endeavour to prevent a recurrence of the painful event.

3.1 Processes and Approaches

The dynamics of cognitive processing in spatial tasks shed light on the nuanced interplay between top-down and bottom-up strategies, mirroring the dichotomy of analytical and holistic approaches elucidated in existing literature [6, 21]. Drawing parallels, top-down processing aligns with analytical strategies, where individuals systematically dissect a given stimulus into discrete components. This methodical deconstruction allows for a meticulous examination of each element, akin to the analytical approach's detailed breakdown in spatial tasks.

Conversely, bottom-up processing echoes the holistic strategies observed in task performance. Holistic approaches thrive on parallel cognitive processes, predominantly driven by visualisation [22]. Similarly, the holistic strategy mirrors the bottom-up processing by embracing a comprehensive perspective that integrates various elements simultaneously, much like how bottom-up processing assimilates information from the sensory input without a predetermined structure [39]. The gender-based distinction in spatial task strategies further reinforces the analogy between top-down/bottom-up processing and analytical/holistic strategies. Females, akin to individuals favouring top-down processing, lean towards analytical strategies. Their preference for systematically breaking down stimuli aligns with the step-by-step approach characteristic of top-down processing. Conversely, males exhibit a preference for holistic cognitive processing, echoing the bottom-up strategy [14, 44, 45]. In tasks like mental rotation tests, males exhibit a reduced reliance on manual manipulation, emphasising mental imagery and parallel cognitive processes, akin to the holistic strategy's simultaneous integration of information.

This cognitive dichotomy provides a comprehensive lens through which to understand the varied strategies individuals employ in spatial tasks. Just as top-down and bottom-up processing illuminate the cognitive pathways in information processing, the analytical and holistic strategies shed light on the divergent yet complementary approaches individuals adopt when confronted with spatial challenges [40, 41]. The intricate interplay between these strategies not only underscores the complexity of cognitive processes but also emphasises the diverse ways individuals navigate and make sense of spatial information. It is important to note, however, that top-down and bottom-up processing are not distinct cognitive processing techniques, nor are they exclusive to a certain gender. In many cases, they work together to optimise cognitive performance.

4 Conclusion

This study has aimed to elucidate the intricate nuances of gender-related cognitive disparities in spatial abilities, with a specific focus on spatial visualisation and mental rotation tasks. The paper explores various aspects of spatial cognition, covering visualisation, rotation, and broader cognitive processes linked to spatial ability. Discerned gender differences, especially in tasks like mental rotation, prompt a comprehensive consideration of contributing factors, spanning biological underpinnings, environmental influences, and sociocultural dimensions. The time component introduced by mental rotation tests adds complexity to interpreting gender disparities. The discovery that such differences diminish without time constraints [14, 24] emphasises the importance of carefully considering testing conditions and methodologies in cognitive research.

This study has shed light on the multifaceted landscape of gender-related differences in spatial cognition within the context of STEM education. Through the exploration of two key research questions, several practical recommendations for future research and implications for the STEM community have been identified. Firstly, further investigation into gender-related differences in spatial cognition is warranted, with a particular emphasis on longitudinal studies and the influence of sociocultural factors. Understanding the developmental trajectories of spatial cognitive abilities in individuals from diverse gender backgrounds can provide valuable insights into potential interventions and support mechanisms. It is essential to acknowledge that, like any test, the mental rotation test is not without its limitations. While providing valuable insights into spatial reasoning abilities, its accuracy may be influenced by factors such as cultural differences, educational background, and individual cognitive styles. Recognising these limitations opens the door to refinement and improvement. Through careful revisions and adjustments, the mental rotation test has the potential to evolve into a highly reliable and valid tool [15]. Researchers and educators can collaborate to enhance its precision and applicability, ensuring that it accurately reflects an individual's spatial cognition.

Secondly, the integration of neurobiological findings into our understanding of cognitive diversity is essential. Utilising advanced imaging techniques and exploring hormonal and genetic influences can deepen our understanding of the neural underpinnings of gender-based variations in spatial cognition, paving the way for more targeted interventions and educational strategies. The implications go beyond theoretical discussion, focusing on the practical applications of the mental rotation test in educational and vocational settings. Its importance in informing instructional strategies and assisting career decisions based on a person's spatial reasoning abilities is paramount. The recognition of cognitive processing differences between males and females, particularly in regard to top-down and bottom-up strategies [24, 40, 41] provides a conceptual framework for understanding the divergent yet complementary approaches used in spatial tasks. The analogy between analytical and holistic strategies [46], as well as the cognitive dichotomy of top-down and bottom-up processing, helps us better understand the intricate interplay within spatial cognition.

Thirdly, this paper underscores the importance of developing educational strategies and interventions that accommodate diverse gender-related spatial cognitive patterns. By incorporating spatial reasoning exercises and providing professional development opportunities for educators, we can create more inclusive learning environments that support the success of all students in STEM fields. In conclusion, addressing the multifaceted nature of gender-related cognitive differences requires a comprehensive and context-aware approach in future research efforts. For instance, employing scaffolded learning approaches, where educators begin with basic concepts and gradually introduce higher-level ideas, aids in building a comprehensive understanding of content for learners. Engaging students in hands-on activities, discussions, and problem-solving tasks encourages both exploration (bottom-up processing) and conceptualisation (top-down processing) through active learning. Through differentiated instruction, educators can tailor teaching strategies and assessment to accommodate diverse learners in their teaching environments, thus fostering equal opportunities for all. This study's findings add to the theoretical understanding of cognitive processes as well as the practical implications for educational and vocational settings. The commitment to Universal Design for Learning in cognitive research calls for continuous refinement of methodologies and interpretations, all guided by the overarching goal of recognising and celebrating the diversity of cognitive abilities across genders [15, 47]. As the academic journey in this field continues, it is critical to create an environment that recognises the richness and variability inherent in individual cognitive profiles, transcending gender-based distinctions.

Disclosure of Interests. The authors have no competing interests to declare that are relevant to the content of this article.

References

1. McNea, M., Cole, R., Tanner, D., Lane, D.: Problematising and framing spatial research in engineering education. Presented at the SEFI 2023 Engineering Education for Sustainability (2023)
2. Sorby, S., Veurink, N., Streiner, S.: Does spatial skills instruction improve STEM outcomes? The answer is "yes." Learn. Individ. Differ. **67**, 209–222 (2018). https://doi.org/10.1016/j.lindif.2018.09.001
3. Stieff, M., Uttal, D.: How much can spatial training improve STEM achievement? Educ. Psychol. Rev. **27**(4), 607–615 (2015). https://doi.org/10.1007/s10648-015-9304-8
4. Shepard, R.N., Metzler, J.: Mental rotation of three-dimensional objects. Science **171**(3972), 701–703 (1971). https://doi.org/10.1126/sci-ence.171.3972.701
5. Birenbaum, M., Kelly, A.E., Levi-Keren, M.: Stimulus features and sex differences in mental rotation test performance. Intelligence **19**(1), 51–64 (1994). https://doi.org/10.1016/0160-2896(94)90053-1
6. Moè, A., Pazzaglia, F.: Following the instructions!: effects of gender beliefs in mental rotation. Learn. Individ. Differ. **16**(4), 369–377 (2006). https://doi.org/10.1016/j.lindif.2007.01.002
7. Hamson, D.K., Roes, M.M., Galea, L.A.M.: Sex Hormones and Cognition : Neuroendocrine influences on memory and learning. https://open.library.ubc.ca/soa/cIRcle/collections/facultyresearchandpublications/52383/items/1.0369058. Accessed 6 June 2023
8. Grimshaw, G.M., Sitarenios, G., Finegan, J.A.: Mental rotation at 7 years: relations with prenatal testosterone levels and spatial play experiences. Brain Cogn. **29**(1), 85–100 (1995). https://doi.org/10.1006/brcg.1995.1269
9. Esipenko, E.A., et al.: Comparing spatial ability of male and female students completing humanities vs. technical degrees. Psychol. Russ. **11**(4), 37–49 (2018). https://doi.org/10.11621/pir.2018.0403
10. Lee, Y., Capraro, R.M., Bicer, A.: Gender difference on spatial visualization by college students' major types as STEM and non-STEM: a meta-analysis. Int. J. Math. Educ. Sci. Technol. **50**(8), 1241–1255 (2019). https://doi.org/10.1080/0020739X.2019.1640398

11. Lane, D., Lynch, R., McGarr, O.: Problematizing spatial literacy within the school curriculum. Int. J. Technol. Des. Educ. **29**(4), 685–700 (2019). https://doi.org/10.1007/s10798-018-9467-y

12. Lane, D., Sorby, S.: Bridging the gap: blending spatial skills instruction into a technology teacher preparation programme. Int. J. Technol. Des. Educ. **32**(4), 2195–2215 (2022). https://doi.org/10.1007/s10798-021-09691-5

13. Hegarty, M., Waller, D.A.: Individual differences in spatial abilities. In: The cambridge handbook of visuospatial thinking, pp. 121–169. Cambridge University Press, New York, NY, US (2005). https://doi.org/10.1017/CBO9780511610448.005

14. Hegarty, M.: Ability and sex differences in spatial thinking: what does the mental rotation test really measure? Psychon. Bull. Rev. **25**(3), 1212–1219 (2018). https://doi.org/10.3758/s13423-017-1347-z

15. Bartlett, K.A., Camba, J.D.: Gender differences in spatial ability: a critical review. Educ. Psychol. Rev. **35**(1), 8 (2023). https://doi.org/10.1007/s10648-023-09728-2

16. Voyer, D., Voyer, S.D., Saint-Aubin, J.: Sex differences in visual-spatial working memory: a meta-analysis. Psychon. Bull. Rev. **24**(2), 307–334 (2017). https://doi.org/10.3758/s13423-016-1085-7

17. Alvarez-Vargas, D., Abad, C., Pruden, S.M.: Spatial anxiety mediates the sex difference in adult mental rotation test performance. Cogn. Res. **5**(1), 31 (2020). https://doi.org/10.1186/s41235-020-00231-8

18. Delage, V., Trudel, G., Retanal, F., Maloney, E.A.: Spatial anxiety and spatial ability: mediators of gender differences in math anxiety. J. Exper. Psychol. General **151**(4), 921–933 (2022). https://doi.org/10.1037/xge0000884

19. Lourenco, S.F., Liu, Y.: The impacts of anxiety and motivation on spatial performance: implications for gender differences in mental rotation and navigation. Curr. Dir. Psychol. Sci. **32**(3), 187–196 (2023). https://doi.org/10.1177/09637214231153072

20. Ramirez, G., Gunderson, E.A., Levine, S.C., Beilock, S.L.: Spatial anxiety relates to spatial abilities as a function of working memory in children. Quar. J. Exper. Psychol. **65**(3), 474–487 (2012). https://doi.org/10.1080/17470218.2011.616214

21. Sorby, S.A.: Educational research in developing 3-d spatial skills for engineering students. Int. J. Sci. Educ. **31**(3), 459–480 (2009). https://doi.org/10.1080/09500690802595839

22. Vandenberg, S.G., Kuse, A.R.: Mental rotations, a group test of three-dimensional spatial visualization. Percept. Mot. Skills **47**(2), 599–604 (1978). https://doi.org/10.2466/pms.1978.47.2.599

23. Caissie, A.F., Vigneau, F., Bors, D.A.: What does the mental rotation test measure? an analysis of item difficulty and item characteristics. Open Psychol. J. **2**(1), 94–102 (2009). https://doi.org/10.2174/1874350100902010094

24. Butler, T., et al.: Sex differences in mental rotation: top–down versus bottom–up processing. Neuroimage **32**(1), 445–456 (2006). https://doi.org/10.1016/j.neuroimage.2006.03.030

25. Host, L., Jansen, P.: The influence of the design of mental rotation trials on performance and possible differences between sexes: A theoretical review and experimental investigation. SAGE Publications (2023).https://journals.sagepub.com/doi/full/10.1177/17470218231200127. Accessed 11 Apr 2024

26. Baddeley, A.: Working memory: looking back and looking forward. Nat. Rev. Neurosci. **4**(10), 829–839 (2003). https://doi.org/10.1038/nrn1201

27. Gardner, H.: Multiple intelligences: the theory in practice. In: Multiple intelligences: the theory in practice, pp. xvi, 304. Basic Books/Hachette Book Group, New York, NY, US (1993)

28. Bors, D.A., Vigneau, F.: Sex differences on the mental rotation test: An analysis of item types. Learn. Individ. Differ. **21**(1), 129–132 (2011). https://doi.org/10.1016/j.lindif.2010.09.014

29. Bartlett, K.A., Dorribo Camba, J.: The role of a graphical interpretation factor in the assessment of Spatial Visualization: a critical analysis. Spatial Cogn. Comput. **23**(1), 1–30 (2023). https://doi.org/10.1080/13875868.2021.2019260

30. Levine, S.C., Foley, A., Lourenco, S., Ehrlich, S., Ratliff, K.: Sex differences in spatial cognition: advancing the conversation. WIREs Cognit. Sci. **7**(2), 127–155 (2016). https://doi.org/10.1002/wcs.1380

31. Toth, A.J., Campbell, M.J.: Investigating sex differences, cognitive effort, strategy, and performance on a computerised version of the mental rotations test via eye tracking. Sci. Rep. **9**(1), 19430 (2019). https://doi.org/10.1038/s41598-019-56041-6

32. Kapoor, R., Fahle, E., Kanopka, K., Klinowski, D., Ribeiro, A., Domingue, B.: Differences in time usage as a competing hypothesis for observed group differences in accuracy with an application to observed gender differences in PISA data (2023). https://doi.org/10.31234/osf.io/6wsmq

33. Ertl, B., Luttenberger, S., Paechter, M.: The impact of gender stereotypes on the self-concept of female students in STEM subjects with an under-representation of females. Front. Psychol. **8** (2017). https://doi.org/10.3389/fpsyg.2017.00703

34. Cheryan, S., Ziegler, S.A., Montoya, A.K., Jiang, L.: Why are some STEM fields more gender balanced than others? Psychol. Bull. **143**(1), 1–35 (2017). https://doi.org/10.1037/bul0000052

35. Kotsopoulos, D., Zambrzycka, J., Makosz, S.: Gender differences in toddlers' visual-spatial skills. Math. Think. Learn. **19**(3), 167–180 (2017). https://doi.org/10.1080/10986065.2017.1328634

36. Uttal, D.H., Cohen, C.A.: Spatial thinking and stem education: when, why, and how?'. In: Ross, B.H. (ed.) Psychology of Learning and Motivation, vol. 57, pp. 147–181. Elsevier Academic Press Inc, San Diego (2012). https://doi.org/10.1016/B978-0-12-394293-7.00004-2

37. Voyer, D., Voyer, S., Bryden, M.P.: Magnitude of sex differences in spatial abilities: a meta-analysis and consideration of critical variables. Psychol. Bull. **117**(2), 250–270 (1995). https://doi.org/10.1037/0033-2909.117.2.250

38. Voyer, D., Rodgers, M.A., McCormick, P.A.: Timing conditions and the magnitude of gender differences on the Mental Rotations Test. Memory Cogn. **32**(1), 72–82 (2004). https://doi.org/10.3758/BF03195821

39. Dietrich, A.: Neurocognitive mechanisms underlying the experience of flow. Conscious. Cogn. **13**(4), 746–761 (2004). https://doi.org/10.1016/j.concog.2004.07.002

40. Sarter, M., Givens, B., Bruno, J.P.: The cognitive neuroscience of sustained attention: where top-down meets bottom-up. Brain Res. Brain Res. Rev. **35**(2), 146–160 (2001). https://doi.org/10.1016/s0165-0173(01)00044-3

41. Ligeza, T., Tymorek, A., Wyczesany, M.: Top-down and bottom-up competition in visual stimuli processing. Acta Neurobiol. Exp. **77**, 305–316 (2017). https://doi.org/10.21307/ane-2017-063

42. Hochstein, S., Ahissar, M.: View from the top: hierarchies and reverse hierarchies in the visual system. Neuron **36**(5), 791–804 (2002). https://doi.org/10.1016/S0896-6273(02)01091-7

43. Bar, M.: A cortical mechanism for triggering top-down facilitation in visual object recognition. J. Cogn. Neurosci. **15**(4), 600–609 (2003). https://doi.org/10.1162/089892903321662976

44. Pletzer, B.: Sex-specific strategy use and global-local processing: a perspective toward integrating sex differences in cognition. Front. Neurosci. **8** (2014). https://doi.org/10.3389/fnins.2014.00425

45. Hsing, H.-W., Bairaktarova, D., Lau, N.: Using eye gaze to reveal cognitive processes and strategies of engineering students when solving spatial rotation and mental cutting tasks. J. Eng. Educ. **112**(1), 125–146 (2023). https://doi.org/10.1002/jee.20495

46. Carroll, J.B.: Human cognitive abilities: a survey of factor-analytic studies. In: Carroll, J.B (ed.) Ergonomics, vol. 38 (1993). https://doi.org/10.1080/00140139508925174
47. Bufasi, E., et al.: Addressing the complexity of spatial teaching: a narrative review of barriers and enablers. Front. Educ. China **9**, 1–16 (2024). https://doi.org/10.3389/feduc.2024.1306189

STEAM (Science, Technology, Engineering, Art, and Mathematics)

Emerging Trajectory for Disembedding: An Online Educational Program for Spatial Thinking in a Context of Visual Arts and Mathematics Education

Mehtap Kus[1]([✉]) [iD] and Nora S. Newcombe[2] [iD]

[1] Aksaray University, 68100 Aksaray, Turkey
mozen@aksaray.edu.tr
[2] Temple University, Philadelphia, PA 19122, USA

Abstract. This study interpreted students' disembedding skills within the intersecting context of visual arts and mathematics, drawing upon studies on psychology, arts, and mathematics education. It aimed to identify an emerging trajectory for disembedding skill development by employing a design-based research methodology and novel interpretation of works of art. The study involved seven sixth grade students, following one-on-one teaching experiments with six students. They participated in an online program to support students' spatial thinking, utilizing GeoGebra Classroom. Video recordings were watched, and students' talks and drawings were analyzed to build an understanding of disembedding. The findings of the study revealed traces of shifts in students' interpretation of works of art through the lens of disembedding. This study could contribute to our understanding of how learners develop spatial thinking in informal learning settings like mathematics and art museums.

Keywords: Disembedding · Spatial Thinking · Visual Arts and Mathematics · Interdisciplinary Education · Informal Learning Settings

1 Introduction

Spatial thinking plays a central role in STEM disciplines as well as other disciplines such as arts, architecture, and graphic design [12]. Recent research on spatial thinking suggests a shift towards studying domain-specific and contextualized spatial thinking skills, unlike the nature of existing psychometric tests [2]. Atit et al. [2] argued that the tasks in psychometric tests lack the complexity of domain-specific problems encountered in STEM fields. For example, in geosciences, Kastens and Ishikawa (2006) argued the differences between disembedding tasks specific to geosciences and tasks like embedding figures test often mentioned in psychology literature. This underscores the need for continued investigation into different types of spatial thinking within each discipline to enrich our understanding of spatial thinking in theory and practice [5].

Disembedding, the spatial thinking skill to encode the shape of objects and find them within a complex or distracting configuration, is considered a crucial skill in both

© The Author(s), under exclusive license to Springer Nature Switzerland AG 2024
M. Živković et al. (Eds.): Spatial Cognition 2024, LNAI 14756, pp. 81–96, 2024.
https://doi.org/10.1007/978-3-031-63115-3_6

visual arts and mathematics education [13]. It is fundamental for dealing with geometric problems [17]. Separating a specific figure from its background and understanding the relations between and within parts and whole is essential in conversations with works of art [3]. Despite its crucial role in both mathematics and visual arts education, disembedding has received less attention from researchers compared to other spatial thinking skills such as mental rotation, particularly in mathematics education [17].

This study aims to explore middle school students' disembedding skills within the intersecting context of visual arts and mathematics. It seeks to identify emerging trajectories of disembedding skill by employing a design-based research methodology [15]. To design theoretically grounded educational activities in the emerging field of interdisciplinary visual arts and mathematics education [7], this study interpreted works of art (e.g., Max Bill), drawing upon relevant research in psychology, arts, and mathematics education [20, 23]. By designing an online learning program utilizing GeoGebra Classroom, this study aimed to contribute to our understanding of how learners develop spatial thinking skills in informal learning settings like mathematics and art museums.

2 Theoretical Background

2.1 Disembedding

Newcombe and Shipley [13] proposed a four-level typology of spatial thinking: intrinsic-static (coding objects' spatial properties), intrinsic-dynamic (transformation of the coding of properties), extrinsic-static (coding objects' spatial location considering the location of other objects or a frame of reference), and extrinsic-dynamic (transforming the relations between objects when one of them or the viewer moves). Disembedding, one of the intrinsic-static skills, was described as encoding of objects' shape and finding shapes in a complex or distracted configuration.

Disembedding skills have been interpreted in diverse domains, including geosciences [6], meteorology [9], and mathematics education [7, 17]. In mathematics education,

Table 1. Developmental progression of children's disembedding skills [17].

Developmental progression	Description
Pre-disembedder	Identifying a single (isolated) shape or small groups of shapes that are separate from others.
Simple disembedder	Identifying the shapes within arrangements where figures overlap (but not embedded shapes) and identifying the frame of complex configurations.
Shapes-in-shape disembedder	Identifying primary structures in complex configurations and embedded figures (e.g., finding a rectangle inside a rectangle)
Secondary structure disembedder	Identifying secondary structures, which play a supportive role in the construction of complex figures.
Complete disembedder	Identifying various possible arrangements in a complex configuration.

Sarama and Clements [17] proposed a five-level developmental progression for disembedding 2D shapes (ages 3–8): pre-disembedder, simple disembedder, shapes-in-shape disembedder, secondary structure disembedder, and complete disembedder. These levels represent increasing ability to identify shapes within shapes and ultimately perceive all possible configurations (Table 1). This progression was interpreted within the interdisciplinary context of visual arts and mathematics.

2.2 Learning to See Visual Displays

Previous research investigated the role of different ways of 'seeing' in arts, design, or mathematics education [7, 14, 18] and how we can learn to see these displays in new ways [14, 19, 20]. Seeing is an active process through which we select and interpret visual information rather than passively receiving it [1]. This process is shaped by our knowledge, expectations, and previous experiences [1, 21, 23]. Wittgenstein [23] provided an example of a change of aspect in a visual display. When someone says, 'Now I am seeing this,' they are not simply reporting a new visual experience; they are describing a new way of understanding the object. Even though the picture itself remains unchanged, the viewer's interpretation has shifted.

Changing ways of seeing can be found in various examples across mathematics, psychology, arts, and design. These include restructured diagrams [18, 22], a shift in perception in Neolithic art from solely patterns to relating patterns with their surroundings, the empty space around them [10]; new perspectives on the Cartesian plane [20]; shifting from only global elements to both local and global ones in mathematical diagrams [19], and perceiving works of art in both 2D and 3D [7]. These studies from psychology, arts, design, and mathematics education inform this study about how we can understand students' shifting perception and support their disembedding skills.

2.3 Learning Arts and Mathematics in Informal Learning Settings

Informal mathematics education offers new perspectives in mathematics education. Nemirovsky et al. [11] described informal learning as, "one in which learners become engaged in questions that matter to them, diversify their sense of what they are capable of, achieve mastery in learning through collaboration, and pursue unanticipated experimentations" (p. 970). Museums are considered one of the crucial informal learning settings. From on-site workshops to innovative online programs like MoMA MOOCs and hybrid blends, museums address a variety of learning styles and preferences. Museums like the National Museum of Mathematics (MoMath) transitioned its programs online, expanding its reach to learners worldwide and filling crucial learning gaps [8]. In this context, this study aims to design an online learning program specifically for middle school students, focusing on the concepts of disembedding, as a crucial skill of spatial thinking. This program utilizes GeoGebra Classroom, a newly developed online platform that allows teachers and students to connect and interact using their devices.

3 Method

This study aimed to design educational activities that foster students' spatial thinking skills, particularly disembedding skill, within the context of interdisciplinary mathematics and visual arts education. To achieve this goal, we employed the Design Based Research (DBR) method, as it facilitates the systematic design, development, and evaluation of educational interventions through iterative and cyclical process [15].

The study involved three cycles (Prototype I, II, and the last implementation). This paper presents the findings from the last implementation.

3.1 Participants

The first cycle (prototype I) involves one-to-one case studies with three sixth-grade students (two females, one male). The second cycle (prototype II) involves one-to-one case studies with three sixth-grade female students. The last cycle was implemented with a group of seven sixth-grade students (four males, three females). Participants were sixth-grade students enrolled in a public school in Turkey who participated in the program remotely. To participate remotely, students needed access to a computer and internet from their homes. The researcher contacted the school principal to identify potential participants who met this requirement. Participants were selected following the principal's guidance and their voluntary assent to participate. Informed consent was obtained from participants' parents who were provided with detailed information about the study. Before conducting study, permissions from the Human Research Ethic Committee and the Turkish Ministry of Education were obtained.

3.2 Design of the Activities

Before designing tasks, minimalist and concrete art movement artists' works of art were collected (e.g., Sol LeWitt, Robert Mangold, Max Bill, Lygia Clark). These works were grouped based on two major categories: arrangement of shapes in the layout (isolated, overlapped, and embedded), and explicitness of the contours (explicit and hidden). This categorization resulted in six sub-categories (Table 2). After the categorization and proto-typing phases, this study primarily focused on the artworks of Max Bill, a Swiss Concrete artist whose work was informed by Gestalt psychology, in which he received training at the Bauhaus School (Gamwell 2016). His artworks are particularly well-suited to hidden figures and embedding figures tests, which rely on Gestalt psychology studies (e.g., Gottschaldt 1938; Wertheimer 1938).

This study involved three major sessions in addition to introduction session. In the introduction session, basic properties of GeoGebra software were introduced. The first session involved works of art with explicit contours or shapes. The second session focused on works of art with hidden contours or hidden shapes. The third session focused on works of art with reversible figures involving line continuation and perceived as both 2D and 3D. After exploring several digital software options, GeoGebra emerged as the most suitable choice due to its unique properties such as engaging with geometry, hiding or manipulating shapes, freehand sketching and tracing shapes from artworks, importing artwork for analysis, and offering an online classroom for collaborative learning and real-time observation of students' work by the teacher or researcher.

The sessions were designed based on previous studies in visual arts, mathematics education, and psychology [7, 16, 19]. This study divided observation of works of art into two parts: *individual observation* and *group observation* of works of art [7]. This approach helps students to observe works of art carefully and go beyond first glance impressions by slowing down their observation process. Students observed the artworks individually in GeoGebra and then discussed them together. During discussions, they used Zoom's annotation tool and GeoGebra's pen tool when granted remote control. We utilized four major methods drawing on the previous studies in order to encourage them for careful and detailed observations: (a) *tracing of geometric shapes* and *talking* about them [19], (b) *guided observation process* (first asking students to find shapes without telling which shapes are represented, then asking students to find a particular shape in the work of art without showing the image of that shape, and lastly asking students find this shape by showing its image if they did not see it); (c) *asking questions that encourage them for careful observation* ('What else do you see or notice?' 'Is there

Table 2. Categorization of works of art.

Design of layout	Explicit	Hidden
Isolated	Shapes are placed separately in the layout. The contours of all shapes are explicitly drawn. Robert Mangold, Four squares within a square, 1974	Shapes are placed separately in the layout. One or more contours of shapes are missing or hidden. Robert Mangold, A square with four shapes cut away from the Rubber Stamp Portfolio, 1976/1977
Overlapped	Shapes can include parts of other shapes, but not all of another shape's parts. The contours of all the shapes are explicitly drawn. Max Bill, Helmhaus Zürich, 1984	Shapes can include parts of other shapes, but not all parts. One or more contours of the overlapped shapes are missing or hidden. Max Bill, 7 scarious portfolio, 1967
Embedded	Shapes are put into other shapes. The contours of all shapes are explicitly drawn. Max Bill, Vier farben gleicher menge, 1970/1972	Shapes are put into other shapes. One or more contours of the shapes are missing or hidden. Lygia Clark, Study for planes in modulated surface, 1957

any shape you haven't noticed before?') and (d) *using different kind of works of art* for developing diverse ways of seeing [7]. The students were instructed to find as many shapes as they can and write/tell their names. During group observation part, students were also encouraged to see *repetition, concatenation* (combinations of identical or different shapes), *embedding* (shapes in shapes), drawing on the study of Sabl'e-Meyer et al. [16] in which they identified basic operations forming the basis of geometric shapes produced by human cultures.

3.3 Data Collection

This study involved four major steps: (1) personal experience, (2) prototype I, (3) prototype II, and (4) last implementation. Students participated in the Zoom meetings from their homes. The sessions were entirely online and video-recorded. Two computers were used for recording sessions. The first computer recorded GeoGebra classroom where students joined each session. This recording helped us observe and analyze the students' actions moment-by-moment during individual observation. The second computer recorded the Zoom meeting where students worked on a shared screen to observe works of art again with their friends and collaboratively trace the shapes they could see. After two initial experiments (Prototype I and II), the video recordings were rewatched, and the sessions were revised. The last implementation was conducted with a group of students in a virtual GeoGebra classroom. During the last implementation, the link for digital classrooms for each session was sent to students at the beginning of the session. The first author, with experience in visual arts and mathematics education, directed the sessions. Each session included two parts: observation of works of art (first day) and reconstruction of works of art (second day). Each part of the sessions took almost one hour and forty-five minutes. This paper presents the findings regarding the first parts of the sessions, observation of works of art, from the last implementation.

3.4 Data Analysis

The developmental progression of disembedding for young children in mathematics education developed by Sarama and Clements [17] provides a base for the development of the initial draft of hypothetical learning trajectory. Constant comparative method [4] was used to illuminate the intricacies of students' disembedding processes within the specific context of visual arts and mathematics. The unit of analysis was students' talks and drawings. Critical events (particularly shifts in their ways of thinking) were determined. Then, each critical event or segment was related to the trajectories proposed by Sarama and Clements [17] and interpreted within the context of the study. Table 3 presents the last version of emerging trajectory for disembedding, drawing upon emerged data, and Sarama and Clements' trajectory [17], and works of art by Max Bill. This learning trajectory, designed for children aged 3–8, aims to foster disembedding in mathematics education. It does not make connections with arts education. The current study interprets this trajectory within the interdisciplinary context of visual arts and mathematics education by adapting the works of art to the context of this study. Considering the grade level (sixth grade, twelve years old) and the nature of the artworks utilized in this current study, the hypothetical trajectory levels are more complex than those of Sarama and Clements (2009). Several changes have been made to the levels, including the addition of the reversible 'figure disembedder' due to the nature of artworks perceived as both 2D and 3D. Furthermore, the 'shapes-in-shapes' level has been subcategorized into 'primary structure disembedder' and 'secondary structure disembedder'.

Table 3. Categorization of works of art.

	Hypothetical trajectory level	Students' thinking and actions
1	Pre-Disembedder	Identifies isolated shapes in situations with minimal distraction (e.g., less segmentation, color use) e.g., *The student identifies the isolated triangles.*
2	Simple Disembedder	Identifies shapes readily visible shapes in artworks with overlapped and embedded design. e.g., *The student identifies the triangles in the overlapped design.*
3.1	Primary Structure Disembedder	Identifies primary structures, the main shapes (hidden or visible) that are important for the artwork's structure, despite distractions like background elements, divisions, or color variations. e.g., *The student identifies squares in the artworks, even though there are many triangles and different colors that might distract them.*
3.2	Secondary Structure Disembedder	Identifies secondary structures (shapes formed by combining other shapes) even when there are distractions or hidden (missing) contours. e.g., *The student identifies trapezoids of different sizes and orientations within the artwork.*
4	Reversible Figure Disembedder	Identifies 3D shapes in artworks, even if they are hidden. The student can also switch between seeing a flat shape (2D) and a 3D shape. e.g., *The student identifies cube and hexagon, even though they are parts of a flat picture.*
5	Complete Disembedder	Analyzes a wide range of shape arrangements within artworks, often employing a systematic and deliberate approach. e.g., *The student divides the artwork into four equal parts and then further divides each part into halves, demonstrating a systematic approach to finding shapes and their combinations.*

4 Findings

The first part briefly describes how the emerging trajectory in Table 3 was developed based on the Prototype I and II studies, considering space limitations. The findings regarding each session in the last implementation were presented. Then, the findings from the last implementation were presented by focusing on students' observation of artworks with explicit shapes (Episode 1), hidden shapes (Episode 2), and reversible shapes (Episode 3).

4.1 Development of Emerging Trajectory for Disembedding

The emerging trajectory (Table 3) stemmed from one-on-one sessions (Prototypes I and II) with six students. In most cases, students directly saw geometric shapes in artworks with non-distracted and distracted backgrounds. These observations were categorized as pre-disembedder (triangles in Fig. 1a) and simple disembedder (rectangles and triangles in Fig. 1b) respectively. Given more time, some students recognized hidden or underlying shapes crucial to the artwork's structure (e.g., rotated squares in Fig. 1c), indicating primary structure disembedder skills. Recognizing shapes like parallelograms, trapezoids or combinations of shapes (parallelograms in Fig. 1b and irregular polygons in Fig. 1d), which were not seen directly, signified secondary structure disembedder level. Furthermore, students grasped 3D shapes in reversible figures only after the researchers' prompt (reversible figure disembedder). Notably, a very small number of students exhibited systematic exploration of various potential shape combinations (complete disembedder). For example, during Prototype I, a student first focused on single triangles in Fig. 2a (last session). She then used language like 'Let's see combinations of shapes now' and 'These are the same when reflecting each of them'. She divided the square into halves (rectangles) and then quarters (four squares), and explored shapes and combinations of shapes within and between squares, exemplifying the complete disembedder (see some parts of her divisions in Fig. 2).

(a)   (b)   (c)   (d)

Fig. 1. (a) Pre-disembedder (triangles), (b) Simple disembedder (triangles and rectangles), (c) Primary structure disembedder (squares), (d) Secondary structure disembedder (combination of triangle and white irregular polygon)

Fig. 2. Systematic division of artwork for exploration of shapes and their combinations

4.2 Findings from the Last Implementation

Episode I. The works of art in this episode included geometric shapes with explicit contours embedded in a distracted background. Students first observed four artworks individually, writing and tracing the shapes they noticed. This was followed by a group observation of each artwork. To encourage deeper observation, they revisited the first artwork (Fig. 3) at the end of the session with clues to reveal unseen shapes. This episode focused on students' initial and subsequent observations regarding the first artwork (Fig. 3b). During individual observation, all students identified rectangles and triangles (*simple disembedder*) in the artwork (Fig. 3), and only one student (S1) also identified square and parallelogram. During group observation, students noticed *primary* and *secondary structures* within the distracted configuration. This process involved students sharing their observations, with the researcher prompting them to find embedded shapes, combination of shapes, and repetitive shapes at different orientations and sizes. Furthermore, the properties of shapes were discussed when students had confusions about them. The conversation between the researcher and students is presented as follows:

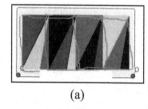   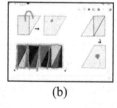   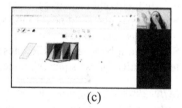

| (a) | (b) | (c) |

Fig. 3. (a) Identification of nested squares in Max Bill's artwork "Untitled, 1973", (b) Exploration of combining shapes to notice new shapes like trapezoids (c) Exploration of nested parallelograms growing larger (screenshot from zoom)

R: Let's take a look at this artwork (1). What shapes do you all see?

S2-S7: Rectangle, triangle.

S1: Parallelogram.

R: Have you seen it before?

S2: No.

S3: Yes, indeed, there is a parallelogram! *(he seems surprised)*

R: S1, can you draw it?

S1: Teacher, there are actually a few more of these (*S1 first draws one parallelogram and then add other two parallelograms next to it*) (1)

(1)

R: Good! Did you all see it? Do you agree with her?

S2-S7: Yes.

R: Can you show rectangles and triangles you said before?

S7: *(draws the outer/frame and the rectangles inside it)* (2) Thereare also smaller ones.

(2)

S5: There are three triangles in each rectangle (*she draws one of them*) (3). Others have it too.

R: Is there anything else you want to add?

(3)

S1: Teacher, there's also a square there *(excitedly talks and draws).* (4)

S2: How?

R: Did you just see it?

S2: Yes, teacher.

(4)

S6: It's like the combination of two rectangles (...)

R: Are there other squares?

S6: There is one right next to the square that S1 just drew *(S1 draws this square)* (5)

(5)

S4: Could it be in the middle ones too? Here, nested together... teacher, all of these squares are nested *(he draws)* (6) (...)

(6)

(After discussion of other works of art, the researcher opens the tasks for guided observation, Figure 3b-c)

R: (...) Are there any shapes formed by the combination of other shapes? Like this one *(demonstrates and explains example)* (7) (...)

(7)

S7: Teacher, there are three or four just like the one you showed...We can combine other shapes to create new shapes, for example, rectangle *(he draws)* (...) (8)

(8)

S5: There are also different types of trapezoids... I found a different trapezoid through the combination of shapes, mmm, two triangles combined *(she draws)* (9) (...) *(students then discuss if it is atrapezoid or not by considering its mathematical properties)*

(9)

Episode II. In this episode, students observed four works of art with hidden shapes. This part presents findings related to one specific artwork (Fig. 4). During individual observation, all students identified isolated shapes, such as triangles (*pre-disembedder*). However, majority of students did not notice primary structures-two hidden concentric squareswithin this artwork. Only one student (S1) noticed the squares and identified a hidden octagon. Following individual observation, students discussed the properties of shapes and discovered new shapes through combining shapes and searching for hidden shapes. The discussion centered on hidden shapes like the squares and octagon, representing primary and secondary structures. Notably, some students struggled with perceiving an empty space as a square. Additionally, they were not sure if the triangles are isosceles or equilateral.

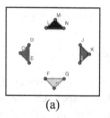 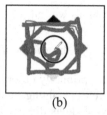 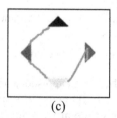
| (a) | (b) | (c) |

Fig. 4. (a) Identification of isolated triangles in Max Bill's artwork (7 scarious portfolio, 1967) during individual observation (pre-disembedding), (b) Identification of hidden squares and octagons during group observation (disembedding of primary and secondary structures), (c) Exploring properties of triangles (equilateral or isosceles)

R: Let's move to this work of art (Fig. 4). Can you tell me what shapes did you see?

S2: Teacher, there is a white square inside (*draws the hidden square in Fig. 4b*). I saw it at first glance.

R: What do you think? Is there a square there?

S6: I don't think so.

S4: If she is referring to the part above the triangles, it is not a perfect square.

S6: Yes, it is empty.

S4: If we don't extend the line outside the triangles (*pointing to the octagon inside, see Fig. 4b*), it wouldn't be a square … It is not a square inside, but it is a square outside (*referring to hidden square standing on one of its corners, see Fig. 4c*).

R: Did everyone notice it at first?

S6: I did not notice it, teacher.

S4: I saw inside first (*referring to octagon, Fig. 4b*), then I saw the triangles.

S2: It could be an octagon inside. I said there was a square inside, but it does not look like a square.

R: Why doesn't it look like a square?

S6: Because of the gap.

S4: If it follows the triangles, it would be [a square], if it doesn't, it [a square] would be the middle part (…)

R: I think you all saw the outer square, but you seemed to see the triangles first. So, what are the properties of the triangles?

S5: Teacher, this time it is isosceles *(they discussed it in previous artwork)*

S6: I think it is equilateral.

R: Why?

S6: Because they are the same, as far as we can see the sides and angles. Each is 60 degrees.

S2: Isn't it 90? It becomes a square like this *(draws the Fig. 4c)* (…)

Episode III. At this episode, students primarily observed artworks that could be perceived as both 2D and 3D, some even containing hidden shapes. During individual observation of the artwork in Fig. 3, students did not identify any 3D shapes. However, they attempted to identify *primary and secondary structures* like parallelograms, rectangles, and squares. Two students even noticed trapezoids. The group observation followed students examining artworks with cubes. This exposure likely influenced their attempts to identify 3D shapes directly in Fig. 3. Additionally, students observed new variations of shapes (primary and secondary structures) by combining existing shapes, even with the artwork's distracted background. Here is a part of the conversation after students realized the presence of a triangular prism:

S5: Teacher, there is something like a rectangular prism here! (*she draws, the green one*) (1)
R: What else? Are there any other 3D shapes here?
S6: Maybe there is, but we can't see it.

(1)

S1: It could also be a hexagon! *[referring to the outer frame of prism, she realized while S5 was tracing the rectangular prism in (1), the green one]*
S5: Yes indeed, it could be rectangular prism and also hexagon.
R: Yeah it could be a hexagon.
S2: Oh, it is a rectangular prism.
S1: But, wouldn't it be a square prism?
R: Is it a square prism or a rectangular prism? (…)
S1: Teacher, isn't this a rectangular prism? (*she draws the pink prism on (1)*)

R: Yes, it is, if we don't think of the surface as a square…it can also be a square prism if its surface is square.
S5: If the bottom and top bases of the prism are square, isn't it a square prism? (*gesturing with her hands*)
R: If all the surfaces are rectangular, we will call it a rectangular prism (...)
S3: Teacher, there are also eight squares, starting the first square with yellow, green, and blue triangles (…)
S2: Here, (*he draws*), there is also a hexagon, teacher, nested hexagons.
R: Great! Did you see them? You said also parallelogram. Can you see parallelograms?
S1-S7: (*S1 and S7 collaboratively draws*) here are parallelograms at different directions, there are so many (*S7 draws the black ones*) (2) …there is a bigger one (*S1 draws the pink ones*) (3).
R: S3 said there are squares. Are they any other squares?
S2: Teacher, there is also a large square made up of the four squares (*he draws nested three squares*) (4)
R: Did you see them?
S3: I saw this for the first time.
R: Okay, S4 wrote on the chat, there is a trapezoid. Can you show it?

(2)

(3)

(4)

(5)

(6)

(7)

S4: I realized that it does not seem like the trapezoid.
R: Well, does anyone see the trapezoid?
S5-S7: (*S5 and S7 collaboratively draws and talks*) teacher, here is a trapezoid (*draws the pink one (5)*), and, a hexagon formed by the combination of trapezoids *(S7 talks and draws black ones) (5)*
R: That's good one! Then, are there any shapes that get bigger and bigger, nested like parallelograms you showed before? Anything else? (…)
S7: It [trapezoid] seems to be stretching from small to large (*he draws smaller and bigger horizontal trapezoids*) (6-7) (…)

5   Conclusion and Discussion

This study aimed to design educational activities for middle school students, drawing upon the studies on psychology, mathematics, and arts education, to support their spatial thinking, particularly disembedding skills. Employing design-based research methodology and a new interpretation of artworks, this study explored students' disembedding of geometric shapes and designed educational tasks in the context of visual arts and mathematics education. The study qualitatively analyzed the traces of shifts in students' interpretation of artworks through the lens of disembedding, particularly drawing on the work of Wittgenstein [23]. Instead of traditional psychometric tests that present a specific target shape within a complex configuration and favor one interpretation over another, this study invited students to explore various interpretations of the configuration, fostering new avenues of perception. The proposed emerging trajectories of disembedding could guide researchers and teachers in understanding students' thinking process within such interdisciplinary programs. It also offers ways to support their disembedding skills such as careful examination of artworks (individual observation followed by group observation), encouraging students to find new shape configurations through guided questions, and discussion on mathematical properties of shapes [7], and asking students to trace the shapes [19].

Episodes 1 and 2 showed students progressing from simple disembedding to primary and secondary structure disembedding during observing specific artworks with friends. For instance, students initially saw rectangles and triangles in the artwork in Fig. 1b. During group observation, they identified additional shapes like squares, parallelograms, and trapezoids. Individual observation allowed us to examine students' initial perceptions. During group observation, if a student noticed a new shape, it prompted others to look for it. Guided questions about shape combinations and variations further encouraged exploration, particularly for secondary shapes they did not initially consider. Additionally, group discussions in Episodes 1 and 2 about isosceles triangles and trapezoids facilitated their recognition in subsequent artworks. This is evident in Episode 3, where students directly noticed trapezoids and combinations forming hexagons, their combinations forming hexagons, without further discussion of properties. Tracing shapes on the screen might have also played a role in triggering them to see shapes, like shapes increasing in size or trapezoid combinations forming hexagons. An example from Episode 3 involves a student tracing a trapezoid, followed by another student recognizing it as part of a hexagon shape. By the final episode, students exhibited a tendency to find primary and secondary structures, indicating a more balanced way of seeing shapes. This likely resulted from their prior discussions on shape properties, the experiences and expectations formed throughout the episodes [1, 23]. The artworks used in this study were diverse, featuring overlapped/embedded figures, explicit/hidden contours, and reversible figures (perceivable as both 2D and 3D). While directly comparing the complexity between these variations is difficult, the designed approach revealed different variations of disembedding skill. It also encouraged students to explore geometric shapes in artworks more richly by prompting them to look beyond first impressions and engage in careful examination.

Future research is needed to refine the proposed trajectory of disembedding and the designed approach through experimental studies. Additionally, researchers should investigate the feasibility of implementing the online program within museum settings. The current study's focus on the formal analysis of artworks, examining geometric shapes and their arrangements, can be broadened in future research to explore additional artistic properties. This might include expressive qualities, like the feeling and meanings conveyed by the artwork, and aesthetical and technical aspects, such as the medium used by the artist. This study contributes to the field by adapting existing psychometric tests for embedded and hidden figures from psychology to the context of interdisciplinary arts and mathematics education. Moving beyond the formal analysis of geometric shapes, this study offers valuable insights for art and mathematics educators. It sheds light on disembedding skill grounded in Gestalt psychology and its connection with figure-ground phenomena within the arts and mathematics context. This provides a valuable case study for art educators, encouraging them to develop their students' shape perception through detailed examination of artworks. By designing an online program and addressing diverse needs and interests of students in mathematics education, this study offers new insights for future research on supporting spatial thinking in informal learning settings like arts and mathematics museums.

Acknowledgments. This study was funded by International Post-Doctoral Research Fellowship Programme of the Scientific and Technological Research Council of Turkey.

Disclosure of Interests. The authors have no competing interests to declare that are relevant to the content of this article.

References

1. Arnheim, R.: Visual thinking. University of California Press, California (1969)
2. Atit, K., Uttal, D.H., Stieff, M.: Situating space: using a discipline-focused lens to examine spatial thinking skills. Cogn. Res. Principl. Implic. **5**(1), 1–16 (2020)
3. Douglas, N.J., Schwartz, J.B., Taylor, J.B.: The relationship of cognitive style of young children and their modes of responding to paintings. Stud. Art Educ. **22**(3), 24–31 (1981)
4. Glaser, B.G., Strauss, A.L.: Discovery of grounded theory: strategies for qualitative research. Routledge, New York (2006)
5. Ishikawa, T., Newcombe, N.S.: Why spatial is special in education, learning, and everyday activities. Cogn. Res. Principl. Implic. **6**(1), 1–5 (2021)
6. Kastens, K.A., Ishikawa, T.: Spatial thinking in the geosciences and cognitive sciences: a cross-disciplinary look at the intersection of the two disciplines. Spec. Pap.-Geol. Soc. Am. **413**, 53–76 (2006)
7. Kus, M., Cakiroglu, E.: Mathematics in the informal setting of art studio: students' visuospatial thinking processes in Studio thinking-based environment. Educ. Stud. Math. **110**(3), 545–571 (2022)
8. Lawrence, C.: A decade of MoMath: TENacity, inTENsity, and poTENtial. math. Intell. **45**, 278–283 (2023)
9. Manduca, C.A., Kastens, K.: Mapping the domain of spatial thinking in the geosciences. Geol. Soc. Am. Spec. Pap. **486**, 45–49 (2012)

10. Metzger, W.: Laws of seeing. The MIT Press, Cambridge (2006)
11. Nemirovsky, R., Kelton, M. L., Civil, M.: Toward a vibrant and socially significant informal mathematics education. In: Cai, J. (ed.) Compendium for research in mathematics education, pp. 90–101. National Council of Teachers of Mathematics, Reston (2017)
12. Newcombe, N.S.: Picture this: increasing math and science learning by improving spatial thinking. Am. Educ. **34**(2), 29–35 (2010)
13. Newcombe, N.S., Shipley, T.F.: Thinking about spatial thinking: new typology, new assessments. In: Gero, J.S. (ed.) Studying visual and spatial reasoning for design creativity, pp. 179–192. Springer, Netherlands (2015)
14. Noble, T., Nemirovsky, R., Dimattia, C., Wright, T.: Learning to see: making sense of the mathematics of change in middle school. Int. J. Comput. Math. Learn. **9**(2), 109–197 (2004)
15. Plomp, T.: Educational design research: an introduction. In: Plomp, T., Nieveen N. (eds.) Educational design research, pp. 11–50. Netherlands Institute for Curriculum Development, Enschede (2013)
16. Sablé-Meyer, M., Ellis, K., Tenenbaum, J., Dehaene, S.: A language of thought for the mental representation of geometric shapes. Cogn. Psychol. **139**, 101527 (2022)
17. Sarama, J., Clements, D.H.: Early childhood mathematics education research: learning trajectories for young children. Routledge, New York (2009)
18. Schön, D.A.: Designing as reflective conversation with the materials of a design situation. Knowl.-Based Syst. **5**(1), 3–14 (1992)
19. Sinclair, N., Moss, J., Hawes, Z., Stephenson, C.: Learning through and from drawing in early years geometry. In: Mix, K. S., Battista, M. T. (eds.) Visualizing mathematics: The role of spatial reasoning in mathematical thought, pp. 229–252. Springer, Cham (2018). https://doi.org/10.1007/978-3-319-98767-5_11
20. Steven, R., Hall, R.: Disciplined perception: Learning to see in technoscience. In: Lampert, M., Blunk, M. L. (eds.) Talking mathematics in school: studies of teaching and learning, pp. 107–150. Cambridge University Press, Cambridge (1998)
21. Wertheimer, M.: In: Ellis, W.D. (ed.) A source book of Gestalt psychology, pp. 71–88. Routledge, England (1938/2007)
22. Wertheimer, M.: Productive thinking. Harper & Brothers Publishers, New York and London (1945)
23. Wittgenstein, L.: Philosophical investigations. Basil Blackwell, Oxford (1986)

The Spatial Aspect of Designing: Opportunities, Challenges, and Conjectures on Engaging Pupils in Spatial Thinking Through Design Education

Caiwei Zhu[✉] [iD] and Remke Klapwijk[iD]

Delft University of Technology, Delft 2628 CJ, The Netherlands
c.zhu-1@tudelft.nl

Abstract. This perspective paper explores the role of spatial thinking in design practices and education by synthesizing insights from qualitative, quantitative, and mixed-methods studies from design education, STEM education, and cognitive psychology. It reviews the mixed results found regarding the relationship between spatial ability and design performance and delves into the intricacies involved in evaluating spatial ability and design ability. To obtain a holistic understanding of the interplay between spatial thinking and design practices, this paper outlines several areas for further exploration, including (1) probing not just expert designers but also young, novice designers' use of spatial thinking in design, (2) examining the nuances in assessing spatial ability and design ability by taking the open-ended nature of design tasks into consideration, and (3) investigating ways to utilize untapped opportunities in design to foster the growth of pupils' spatial and design abilities, enabling them to create innovative and functional solutions to real-world STEM challenges. Furthermore, this paper highlights the interdisciplinary nature of design that can be leveraged to develop pupils' spatial thinking alongside other cognitive skills, generate transferable knowledge applicable to other disciplines, and contribute to the multifaceted discussion on spatial thinking's role in STEM learning.

Keywords: spatial ability · STEM education · design education · K-12 education

1 Introduction

The capacity to turn our creative visions into designs and technologies has been a transformative force throughout history [1]. Essentially, design means conceptualizing and actualizing new entities [2]. It involves processes such as defining and redefining problems, understanding users' needs, making prototypes through various mediums, and developing, testing, and iterating on prototypes. Numerous studies have underscored the importance of design in general education [2–5], and its growing prominence in primary and secondary curricula worldwide is evident in regions such as Europe [4, 6], North America [7], and Asia [8].

In the dynamic and iterative process of designing—where the minds and the hands interact together to shape ideas and products—designers make use of tools and skills,

M. Živković et al. (Eds.): Spatial Cognition 2024, LNAI 14756, pp. 97–113, 2024.
https://doi.org/10.1007/978-3-031-63115-3_7

such as problem framing [9], context mapping for user research [10], analogical thinking [11, 12], sketching [13, 14], as well as spatial thinking [15–17] to create designs that are innovative, relevant, and meaningful to industries and societies. Whether it is designing and engineering increasingly efficient water pumps or sawmills, Ferguson [18] argued that 'thinking with pictures' and imagining the assembly and alterations of objects and elements in minds are inherent in these practices. Historically, scientists, engineers, designers, and technologists frequently leveraged these types of nonverbal thoughts. As Cross [2] outlined, one of the core design abilities involves using 'nonverbal, graphic/spatial modelling media' (p. 20), demonstrating the longstanding role of visual-spatial thinking in design practices and design education.

A substantial body of research has highlighted the important role spatial thinking plays in learning science, technology, engineering, and mathematics (STEM) [19–22] emphasizing the need to develop K-12 pupils' spatial abilities [23]. Further studies suggest that cultivating K-12 pupils' and college students' spatial abilities can lead to improved subject learning outcomes, such as in mathematics [24–26], engineering [27], and chemistry [28]. Less is known about whether a similarly important relationship exists between spatial thinking and design learning.

Learning through design stimulates integrated STEM learning experiences, as design problem-solving often requires engineering practice, technology literacy, mathematical reasoning, and scientific knowledge [29, 30], while also actively engaging spatial thinking [31, 32]. Exploring how K-12 pupils' spatial abilities may be related to their design ability appears to be a relevant topic of investigation. Such research could provide insights into enhancing pupils' design ability by improving their spatial abilities and illustrate how design education could serve as a platform to cultivate pupils' spatial skills.

In this perspective paper, we synthesize findings from studies in design and education that concern the role of spatial thinking in designing. By integrating insights from qualitative, quantitative, and mixed-methods studies, we aim to offer a comprehensive understanding of the intricate relationship between spatial ability and design ability. Additionally, we address the complications that arise from assessing spatial ability and evaluating design ability and identify opportunities for further investigations.

2 How Expert and Novice Designers Use Spatial Thinking in Designing

A number of design studies have provided qualitative or mixed-methods evidence on how designers use their spatial thinking in the process of designing, especially in problem exploration, idea emergence, and sketching to attend to details and make iterations.

Cross [2] detailed the thought processes of a few expert designers in design problem-solving. For instance, to design 'a carrying/fastening device that would enable you to fasten and carry a backpack on a mountain bicycle' (p. 64), one experienced designer first explored and analyzed the design problem by visualizing the problem context in mind and visualizing himself or a rider in the biking scenario. By imagining the different movements performed by the rider going up and downhill, as well as the possible positions where the backpack could be attached in this dynamic process, the designer actively visualized from different perspectives and considered the spatial positions and relations between the rider, the bike, and the environment. Following problem exploration, the emergence of a new design idea, such as perceiving an ambiguous form of a new product in one's mind and continuing to conceptualize it into a more concrete mental image, can be the result of a series of interactions between perception, visual memory and imagery, mental imagery and transformation, and visual representations [33]. Then, to externalize mental images of ideas, designers typically sketch down preliminary ideas and concepts. This practice allows expert designers to attend to the visual details of their ideas, through which they can discover and utilize the spatial and functional relations entailed to generate new ideas or iterations, or to reconfigure and rearrange the visual-spatial elements [34].

Novice designers, such as K-12 pupils, also utilize spatial thinking in design processes. In architecture design projects, such as planning cities and building playgrounds, pupils are often immersed in the experiences of different forms of spaces, which require them to carefully consider and effectively utilize space and spatial relations to satisfy the needs of different groups of people [35–37]. Other design and maker projects may have a stronger focus on the use of technology, such as primary school pupils engaging in virtual 3D makerspace [38] or secondary school pupils making use of 3D modeling tools [39, 40], challenging their ability to visualize and create 3D representations of their ideas using computer-aided design tools. Design projects that emphasize hands-on tinkering and iteration, such as secondary school pupils designing, building, and testing functional windmills [41], and primary school pupils using tangible objects to represent number-space mapping [42], also recruit various practices of spatial thinking, such as visualization, spatial transformations, and spatial motor movements. In addition, in engineering design activities, secondary school pupils used spatial thinking to visualize creative solutions to engineering problems, meanwhile actively using language, sketches, gestures, and hands-on interactions with objects to facilitate their spatial understandings and enrich their visuo-spatial representations [16].

Based on these studies, it is evident that spatial thinking plays a role in the dynamic process of designing, at various design steps and stages, including problem exploration, idea sketching, hands-on and 3D modeling, as well as testing and iterating. Meanwhile, design encompasses a variety of knowledge and skills that are domain-general, such as sketching and modeling, which are not only vital in design but also broadly applicable in other disciplines, such as technology and engineering.

3 The Intricate Relationship Between Spatial Ability and Design Ability

Studies investigating the direct link between students' spatial abilities and their design ability have been relatively scarce and yielded mixed results. A few studies reported a positive correlation between spatial abilities and design performance. For example, Chang [43] studied 12th-grade high school students and found a moderately positive correlation ($r(347) = .351, p < 0.05$) between their spatial ability and their creative performance in a computer-aided design project. Notably, this investigation revealed small to moderate positive correlations between all subscales of spatial abilities (stereo- spatial orientation, plane-spatial orientation, spatial relationship, and spatial perception) with all subscales of creative performance (novelty, aesthetics, and functionality). Chang [43] also found significant differences in these students' creative performance in computer-aided design between students with the highest 27% spatial ability scores and those with the lowest 27% scores ($F = 205.53, p < 0.01$), with a small to medium effect size ($d = 3.02$).

In the context of higher education, Sutton and Williams [44] found significant correlations between first-year design students' achievements in a graphics course and a range of subscores from a spatial test, such as visualization ($r(177) = .23, p < 0.05$) and 2D-3D recognition ($r(177) = .24, p < 0.05$). Suh and Cho [17] found that third-year interior design students' domain-specific spatial ability scores—measured by the Interior Design Domain-specific Spatial Ability Test—positively correlated with the 3D volumetric exploration score they received for their design work ($r(37) = .36, p < 0.05$). Specifically, the domain-specific spatial visualization score correlated positively with both the 3D volumetric exploration scores and the 3D spatial richness scores in design. Finally, investigating the relationship between design performance and designers' general intelligence, Nazidizaji and colleagues [45] found that the architecture students' final year design studio performance correlated positively with their scores on Raven's Progressive Matrices test—a test that requires visual-spatial reasoning and visual analogical reasoning ($r(67) = .26, p < 0.05$).

On the other hand, Allen [46] and Cho [47] found no significant correlation between the spatial abilities scores and undergraduate design students' performance in the design studio or projects. These varying outcomes could be attributed to the small sample size or the differences in methodologies, including diverse measures of spatial abilities and the complexities involved in assessing the qualities of design or designers' capabilities. Future research is necessary to further explore the relationship between spatial abilities and design ability, particularly considering the different levels of design experience and the specific contributions of various components of spatial abilities to design performance.

3.1   Enhancing Spatial Ability Through Design Education

In addition to some of the evidence suggesting a correlation between spatial abilities and design performance, design education also seems to benefit the development of spatial abilities. For example, 6th-graders who participated in six computer-aided design sessions, where they designed objects or places such as 3D homes, cars, playgrounds, and cities, made improvements in spatial visualization, mental rotation, and cross- section visualization tests [48]. Design training also holds the promise of benefiting the development of large-scale spatial skills, such as spatial orientation. Carbonell-Carrera et al. [49] found significant improvement in Perspective Taking Spatial Orientation Test performance ($p < .001$) among college engineering students who participated in a three-day workshop focusing on infrastructure and urban design. In contrast, those who did not attend the workshop showed minor and non-significant improvements in the spatial orientation test.

Similarly, college students who participated in design courses, which involved learning about idea sketching, engineering drawing, creating models, and computer-aided 3D design, demonstrated significant improvements in their spatial visualization skills ($t(127)$

$= 6.07, p < .01$) and understanding of spatial relations ($t(127) = 2.88, p < .05$) [50]. By contrast, those who did not study courses in design showed no statistically significant change in their spatial scores. Interestingly, Lin's study revealed that design students tended to adopt holistic strategies to approach spatial problems, suggesting that they likely visualized the whole objects undergoing spatial transformation in their minds. The holistic approach is generally regarded as a more efficient [51, 52] and more accurate [53] way to solve spatial problems. Students in non-design disciplines, however, adopted analytical strategies more often, suggesting that they might have taken extra steps to count or dissect a complex spatial problem into familiar forms [54], which is comparatively less efficient [52, 53]. This finding raises conjectures about whether design, which frequently involves mentally visualizing and manipulating forms and structures, may help students practice and master the holistic approach to spatial problems, thereby enhancing their efficiency in spatial thinking and spatial problem-solving. Future spatial training might leverage the opportunities presented by various design processes and projects to help students harness strategies to visualize and holistically transform images in their minds when solving spatial tasks.

4 Questions to be Addressed

4.1 The Unclear Relationship Between Designers' Spatial Ability and Design Ability

The inconsistent findings from quantitative examinations on the relationship between spatial abilities and design ability may be partly attributed to the complexities involved in measuring these abilities. To measure design ability, studies have employed distinct approaches: some focused primarily on the end-design product [17, 46], others considered both the design process and the end product [4, 47], and some evaluated the entire design course grade [44]. Besides, these studies adopted different definitions for 'good' or 'creative' designs. Additional concerns have been raised regarding the validity of the design tasks used to measure design performance. For instance, Allen [46] pointed out that the design task used in their study might not have adequately assessed design creativity due to a lack of clear success criteria. Altogether, future studies should be mindful of the inherent complexities of assessing design ability and clearly justify their selected measures to determine students' or pupils' design ability.

Regarding spatial abilities, there has long been a debate on whether a spatial ability test necessarily measures spatial ability. Many have argued that spatial abilities measures are often complicated by other cognitive [55], social [56], or performance factors, such adeptness in using test-taking strategies [53].

The types of stimuli used in spatial ability measures may further result in biases in comprehending and responding to these tests [57–59]. Others have pointed out that existing spatial ability tests do not sufficiently address all the spatial skills needed for solving spatially complex STEM problems [60, 61]. In Suh and Cho's [17] study, college students' design performance correlated only with domain-specific spatial ability tasks, which were more familiar and relevant to the field of design in which those students were studying, but not with the general spatial ability test. This complexity may arise from students relying more on their domain knowledge to solve domain-specific spatial tasks than their general spatial abilities. Thus, it is reasonable to presume that the variations in the types of spatial ability measures used may have contributed to the unclear relationship between designers' spatial ability and design ability.

Potential Influences of Expertise Level

Additionally, previous research has suggested that spatial thinking skills may be more predictive of learners' academic performance in the early stages of learning [62]. However, as learners progress in their education, they tend to depend less on general cognitive abilities such as spatial skills and rely more on specialized knowledge within their specific domains. Notably, many of the aforementioned studies focused on college design students, who have already undergone some design training. It is reasonable to suspect that spatial abilities may not serve as a strong predictor of design performance at this level, given the domain-specific knowledge these students have acquired. To our knowledge, very few studies have examined the relationship between spatial abilities and design ability among K-12 pupils, who typically have little to no design training. The relationship between spatial abilities and design ability among these younger learners warrants further investigation.

4.2 The Distinctions Between Typical Spatial Test Problems and Open-Ended Design Problems

When discussing the spatial aspect of design education, it is important to highlight that designers' ways of problem-solving are arguably different from those in natural or social sciences [2, 63]. This difference primarily stems from design problems being ill-defined and open-ended, necessitating both divergent and convergent thinking [2, 64–66]. In contrast, problems that prioritize using an analytical approach to identify the single best solution involve mainly convergent thinking. Researchers like Cropley and Cropley [3], who have contributed greatly to the field of understanding and evaluating creativity in STEM, suggested that intelligence test questions typically emphasize accuracy and correctness, thus predominantly reflecting convergent thinking. Unlike intelligence tests, which have a stronger emphasis on 'being accurate and correct,' 'homing in on the single best answer,' Cropley and Cropley argued that designers need divergent thinking to 'shift perspectives on existing information (seeing it in a new way) or transforming it,' thereby producing 'alternative or multiple solutions' and developing products that differ from those that existed before (p. 67). For example, when tasked with designing wind-resistant camping gear inspired by nature in a design project, pupils aged 11 to 12 came up with diverse and unconventional solutions that took what was known one step further [67].

It is worth conjecturing that designers employ problem-solving strategies that have nuanced differences from those used to solve analytical problems [2, 3, 67]. Building on Zhu and colleagues' [67] hypotheses that certain aspects of spatial thinking may be unique to the design process and are neither assessed nor developed in conventional spatial tasks or training, we suggest that understanding and, consequently, enhancing spatial abilities through design education requires recognizing the two distinctions between typical spatial test problems and open-ended design problems.

Choosing from Given Options Versus Generating Multiple Solutions

Creative and divergent thinking cannot be measured by choosing from pre-defined answers. Well-known creativity measures such as the Alternate Uses Task [65] and the Torrance Tests of Creative Thinking [68] all value the ability to generate many original and varied solutions. Similarly, design problems, like many real-world problems, do not offer predetermined solutions to choose from; instead, they require divergent idea generation before one can arrive at a potentially fitting solution.

Contrarily, many spatial ability assessments predominantly feature well-defined and close-ended questions. In a majority of diagnostic spatial ability tests, including the widely used ones on mental rotation [69] and the Purdue Spatial Visualization Test [70], as well as more recent tests with educational values like the Spatial Reasoning Instrument [71] and the Mental Folding Test for Children [72], test-takers are provided with a limited number of options and are expected to identify only one or two correct answers. An example of a mental rotation question involving 2D objects from the Spatial Reasoning Instrument is illustrated in Fig. 1.

The figure below shows the picture of a bike.

Which one of the following shows a rotation of the picture?

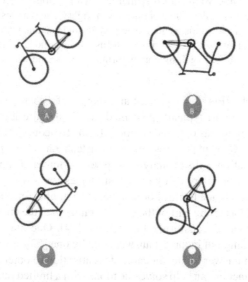

Fig. 1. A mental rotation question from the Spatial Reasoning Instrument [71]. The correct answer is D.

Designers, however, bring what has not yet been made or seen before into reality [73], meaning that they engage in imagining and creating a multitude of options in their minds. Envisioning and developing an array of hazy mental representations of ideas in their minds is different from choosing from a set of visible options on paper or screen. In Fig. 2, we present two examples created by us to illustrate the differences between these two forms of problem presentations.

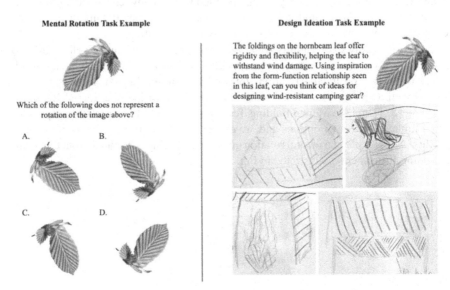

Fig. 2. Spatial tasks. *Note.* Well-defined spatial task with options given (left) and ill-defined, open-ended design ideation task without options given (right). The four design ideas were created by a team of two 12-year-old pupils, including an easy-to-fold tent that withstands wind, a cycling suit with folding design on its surface to protect the user from wind, a foldable shield to preserve campfire, and a table with folding design on its surface to withstand wind.

On the left panel of Fig. 2, we present an example of a spatial task that mimics how 2D mental rotation tasks are typically presented: an initial figure accompanied by several rotated or reflected figures as options to choose from. To deduce that option C cannot be achieved through rotation but requires reflection instead, one would primarily use mental rotation and visualization skills to analyze the given options and converge on the correct answer. Additionally, there are many known strategies for solving typical spatial tasks presented in multiple-choice forms. For instance, one might concentrate on envisioning the transformation of a certain part of the stimuli, rather than the entire stimuli, to reduce the complexity of mental transformation required [74]. One may also use test-taking strategies such as ruling out incorrect answers one by one [53] or focusing on verifying a potentially correct answer while allocating less attention to other options [75].

Although these tactics can help solve questions with a limited range of given options, their applicability may not extend to open-ended prompts, which usually require respondents to generate and manipulate a range of possibilities through both mental and visual representations. On the right panel of Fig. 2, we showcase pupils' design ideas for wind-resistant camping gear inspired by the folding structures on hornbeam leaves. These 12-year-olds visualized four different ways to incorporate the visual-spatial features seen on hornbeam leaves into creative design ideas. Generating and externalizing ideas that do not yet exist in real life reflects the rich visual imagery and non-rigid spatial transformation occurring in their minds. Therefore, while spatial thinking is needed to address both types of problems presented in Fig. 2, solving the design problem likely demands a broader retrieval of mental images as well as a more creative application of spatial transformation and visualization.

Identifying Correct Solutions Versus Seeking Iterations on Solutions

In typical spatial tasks as well as many common assessment questions in mathematics or science, once a predetermined solution is identified, there is often no need for improving on that solution. However, in design, iteration is strongly encouraged and often deemed necessary [4, 76, 77]. After ideating multiple solutions, designers do not simply settle on a desirable one. Instead, they iteratively make improvements to and further elaborate on that solution. In Fig. 3, we present an example where another team of two 12-year-old pupils designed a camping tent that aims not only to withstand wind but also to channel and recycle water, inspired by the spiral-grained trunk of the Whitebark Pine.

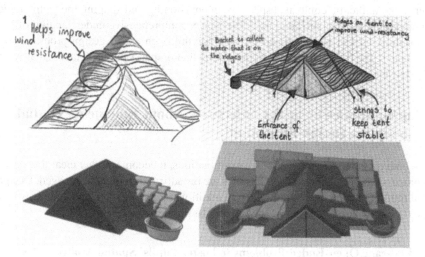

Fig. 3. An example of two 12-year-old pupils iterating and seeking improvements on a design solution.

As these pupils sketched down their idea, they noticed that they needed to specify the side of the entrance and consider additional features to enhance the stability of the tent. Visualizing how their design would be used in real life in their minds, they noticed that the spiraling design would direct rainwater in a certain way. This observation led them to iterate by attaching buckets to the tent to collect the water for other uses. When they made their 3D model on a computer-aided design platform, they further encountered the challenge of determining the optimal spatial positioning of the spiral designs to channel water into the attached buckets. It appears that these pupils perceived and analyzed not only the static spatial structures but also the dynamic properties of and relationships between objects, which is an important process of spatial thinking [78]. Furthermore, these processes align with Suwa and Tversky's [34] description of how designers often discover emerging visual-spatial properties and attend to the spatial and functional relations from their initial sketches, thereby iterating on their initial ideas. Importantly, these improvements are not based on predetermined options but are driven by the many possibilities that designers imagine, envision, and manipulate in their minds.

To summarize, while designers use fundamental spatial skills such as mental rotation and spatial visualization to imagine possible design configurations and improvements, the way they employ these skills and their underlying objectives might differ from how these skills are used in completing typical spatial tests. Presently, assessments of spatial abilities and the design of spatial training might not fully account for these nuanced differences, and the construct of spatial thinking does not yet adequately reflect the creative use of spatial skills. Hence, outcomes from existing spatial ability tests may not adequately reflect respondents' ability to use spatial skills in addressing open-ended, real-world design problems.

Learning from how designers use spatial thinking could be valuable to the field of spatial abilities research, as it adds to the discussion on applying spatial thinking in diverse and authentic contexts, especially in envisioning and shaping the technologies and environments that surround us. Moreover, a comprehensive understanding of how spatial thinking can be developed through solving open-ended design problems may contribute to the formulation of spatial training that prepares pupils to tackle real-world STEM problems.

5   Opportunities for and Conjectures About Enhancing Spatial Ability via Design Education

From both quantitative and qualitative examinations, it becomes rather clear that design is a process where a variety of spatial skills are broadly and frequently engaged. Design-based thinking and practices may offer an additional lens to understand and investigate pupils' use of spatial thinking in solving STEM problems.

5.1   Leverage Open-Ended Problems to Foster Pupils' Spatial Ability and STEM Learning

Education researchers have long emphasized the importance of authentic learning experiences that make use of ill-defined, open-ended, and real-world problems [79, 80]. Increasing efforts have been made to celebrate creativity, divergent thinking, and real-world problem-solving in STEM, such as engaging pupils in solving open-ended mathematics problems [81], integrating open-ended design challenges and design-based practices in learning physics [82], life science [83], and chemistry [84, 85]. For instance, 6th graders testing out and seeking improvements on artificial lung designs exemplified how the iterative nature of design facilitated the consolidation and enactment of content knowledge of the respiratory system [83]. For another example, in developing and evaluating design prototypes of long-lasting soap bubbles through trial and error, 10th graders exercised structure-property reasoning as well as micro-macro thinking, both of which are crucial to chemistry learning [84]. Whether it was visualizing the relationships between different components of the respiratory system, or envisioning the structural features of a soap molecule, it is rather clear that spatial thinking was involved.

Similarly, in the field of spatial abilities research, much research has also underscored the need to develop pupils' spatial abilities through authentic, real-world problems [22, 86, 87]. As the National Research Council [78] in the U.S. described, spatial thinking can be understood as 'using the properties of space as a vehicle for structuring problems, for finding answers, and for expressing solutions' (p. 3). Design education, which emphasizes solving authentic, real-world problems, appears to benefit pupils' spatial skills development such as in spatial visualization, spatial orientation, and understanding of spatial relations [48–50]. Design-based thinking and practices thus appear to be one promising approach to bridge spatial interventions and authentic STEM learning experiences. Future research may consider exploring (1) the potential of incorporating open-ended design problems into spatial intervention and training, (2) how engaging in design training and design-based activities may help learners harness certain spatial thinking strategies, such as adopting the holistic approach to solving spatial problems, and (3) educational approaches to equip learners with the necessary spatial skills that allow them to effectively represent, test out, and iterate on ideas on 2D and 3D mediums by hand or through technologies, leading to novel and functional solutions to real-world design and STEM problems.

5.2 The Varied Cognitive Skills and Interdisciplinary Knowledge Utilized in Design

An examination of spatial thinking in the design context may open up possibilities of training spatial thinking along with other reasoning skills. Besides spatial skills, the design process recruits a range of other cognitive skills, such as divergent and convergent thinking [64], analogical thinking [12], mental imagery [15], working memory [88], and empathy [89]. For example, brainstorming and imagining a range of possible solutions may require divergent thinking, mental imagery, analogical thinking, and working memory, in conjunction with spatial skills. Future research may want to investigate how designers utilize spatial skills alongside other cognitive skills to formulate design solutions, how these cognitive skills may interact with one another, and to what extent different cognitive skills contribute to the quality of a design product, the effectiveness of a design process, and the ability of a designer.

Design performance can also be complicated by factors such as personal and domain-specific knowledge, experience, and skills [90]. One may need to take into consideration learners' previous knowledge in designing, as well as their cognitive beliefs, affective states, self-efficacy, and level of motivation related to design [91]. Additionally, the process of designing inherently embodies constant interactions between the hand and the mind [4] before design ideas are externalized through sketches, drawings, and tangible or virtual artifacts. Therefore, one's proficiency in sketching and making, as well as their self-perceived competence in these skills, may impact their design processes or design outcomes. For example, Alias et al. [92] found that engineering students' tendency to use sketching and drawing positively correlated with their spatial visualization abilities. Thus, it may be worthwhile to take attitudes toward sketching and drawing into consideration when unpacking the relationship between spatial abilities and design ability.

Besides, design as a subject is highly interdisciplinary, drawing from and integrating various types of knowledge and skills from different subjects [73]. Design-based thinking and practices are frequently utilized in the search for innovative and suitable solutions to real-world problems related to science, technology, engineering, or humanities [4]. Meanwhile, learning about and through design holds the potential to generate transferable knowledge applicable to other disciplines. For instance, Levin and Verner [93] organized a ten-hour 3D design and printing workshop, where 7th-grade pupils designed a spinning toy that fits into a Kinder Surprise Egg on a computer-aided design platform and carried out mathematical analyses on the geometrical and mechanical properties of their designs. They found that this design project exercised pupils' design problem-solving and real-world problem-solving skills, use of mathematical language, and their analytical thinking and applied mathematical thinking. Additionally, Bicer and colleagues [94] found that learning about and enacting 3D computer-aided design in a two-week summer camp helped high school students of different gender and ethnic backgrounds develop a more positive perception of the importance of creativity and problem-solving skills in STEM. It appears that the versatile nature of design presents a unique opportunity to cultivate not just spatial skills but also domain-specific and domain-general knowledge and skills for STEM learning.

6 Concluding Remarks

An exploration of spatial thinking in design goes beyond theoretical inquiries—it invites us to reimagine educational practices by intertwining spatial thinking with creative and authentic problem-solving, as well as interdisciplinary learning. A key motivation for enhancing pupils' spatial abilities is the broad and frequent application of spatial skills in STEM learning [22, 95–97]. This paper underscores that spatial skills can be developed not only through analytical STEM problems but also through open-ended STEM problems that require both divergent and convergent thinking. It offers an alternative perspective for examining the use of spatial thinking in solving real-world STEM problems. The ongoing discussions about the relationship between pupils' spatial abilities and design ability, and the potential use of open-ended, real-world problems to challenge and develop pupils' spatial abilities, could benefit various stakeholders, including researchers in cognitive psychology and educational sciences, as well as design researchers, practitioners, and educators.

Acknowledgments. This research is part of SellSTEM-Spatially Enhanced Learning Linked to STEM-Marie Skłodowska-Curie Innovative Training Network to investigate the role of spatial ability in and for STEM learning. It has received funding from the European Union's Horizon 2020 research and innovation programme under the Marie Skłodowska-Curie grant agreement (grant number 956124).

Disclosure of Interests. The authors declare that the research was conducted in the absence of any commercial or financial relationships that could be construed as a potential conflict of interest.

References

1. Klapwijk, R., Stables, K.: Design learning: pedagogic strategies that enable learners to develop their design capability. In: Gill, D., Irving-Bell, D., McLain, M., Wooff, D. (eds.), Bloomsbury handbook of technology education, pp. 271–289. Bloomsbury Publishing (2023)
2. Cross, N.: Designerly ways of knowing, pp. 1–13. Springer London (2006)
3. Cropley, A.J., Cropley, D.: Fostering creativity: a diagnostic approach for higher education and organizations. Hampton Press, Cresskill, NJ (2009)
4. Kimbell, R., Stables, K.: Researching design learning: issues and findings from two decades of research and development (2007)
5. Lewis, T.: Creativity in technology education: providing children with glimpses of their inventive potential. Int. J. Technol. Des. Educ. **19**, 255–268 (2009)
6. Lin, T., Buckley, J., Gumaelius, L., Ampadu, E.: Situating spatial ability development in the Craft and Technology curricula of Swedish compulsory education. In: The 40th international pupils' attitudes towards technology conference proceedings, vol. 1 (2023)
7. Goldman, S., Carroll, M., Royalty, A.: Destination, imagination & the fires within: design thinking in a middle school classroom. In: Proceedings of the seventh ACM conference on Creativity and cognition, pp. 371–372 (2009)
8. Koh, J.H.L., et al.: Design thinking and education, pp. 1–15. Springer Singapore (2015)
9. Schön, D.: The Reflective Practitioner, Temple-Smith, London, UK (1983)
10. Visser, F.S., Stappers, P.J., Van der Lugt, R., Sanders, E.B.: Contextmapping: experiences from practice. CoDesign **1**(2), 119–149 (2005)
11. Gordon, W. J.: Synectics: the development of creative capacity, harper and brothers. New York, NY, USA (1961)
12. Hey, J., Linsey, J., Agogino, A.M., Wood, K.L.: Analogies and metaphors in creative design. Int. J. Eng. Educ. **24**(2), 283 (2008)
13. Purcell, A.T., Gero, J.S.: Drawings and the design process: a review of protocol studies in design and other disciplines and related research in cognitive psychology. Des. Stud. **19**(4), 389–430 (1998)
14. Tversky, B., et al.: Sketches for design and design of sketches. Human Behaviour in Design: Individuals, Teams, Tools, pp. 79–86 (2003)
15. Kavakli, M., Gero, J.S.: Sketching as mental imagery processing. Des. Stud. **22**(4), 347–364 (2001)
16. Ramey, K.E., Uttal, D.H.: Making sense of space: distributed spatial sensemaking in a middle school summer engineering camp. J. Learn. Sci. **26**(2), 277–319 (2017)
17. Suh, J., Cho, J.Y.: Linking spatial ability, spatial strategies, and spatial creativity: a step to clarify the fuzzy relationship between spatial ability and creativity. Thinking Skills and Creativity, vol. 35 (2020)
18. Ferguson, E.S.: The Mind's Eye: Nonverbal Thought in Technology: " Thinking with pictures" is an essential strand in the intellectual history of technological development. Science **197**(4306), 827–836 (1977)
19. Buckley, J., Seery, N., Canty, D.: A heuristic framework of spatial ability: a review and synthesis of spatial factor literature to support its translation into STEM education. Educ. Psychol. Rev. **30**(3), 947–972 (2018)
20. Kell, H.J., Lubinski, D., Benbow, C.P., Steiger, J.H.: Creativity and technical innovation: spatial ability's unique role. Psychol. Sci. **24**, 1831–1836 (2013)
21. Wai, J., Lubinski, D., Benbow, C.P.: Spatial ability for STEM domains: aligning over 50 years of cumulative psychological knowledge solidifies its importance. J. Educ. Psychol. **101**(4) (2009)

22. Zhu, C., et al.: Fostering spatial ability development in and for authentic STEM learning. Front. Educ. **8**, 1138607 (2023)

23. Newcombe, N.: Harnessing Spatial Thinking to Support STEM Learning. OECD Education Working Papers, No. 161. OECD Publishing (2017)

24. Hawes, Z.C., Gilligan-Lee, K.A., Mix, K.S.: Effects of spatial training on mathematics performance: a meta-analysis. Develop. Psychol. **58**(1) (2022)

25. Gilligan, K.A., Thomas, M.S., Farran, E.K.: First demonstration of effective spatial training for near transfer to spatial performance and far transfer to a range of mathematics skills at 8 years. Develop. Sci. **23**(4) (2020)

26. Sorby, S.A., Veurink, N.: Preparing for STEM: impact of spatial visualization training on middle school math performance. J. Women Minorities Sci. Eng. **25**, 1–23 (2019)

27. Sorby, S.A.: Educational research in developing 3-D spatial skills for engineering students. Int. J. Sci. Educ. **31**, 459–480 (2009)

28. Stieff, M.: Improving representational competence using molecular simulations embedded in inquiry activities. J. Res. Sci. Teach. **48**, 1137–1158 (2011)

29. Fan, S.C., Yu, K.C.: How an integrative STEM curriculum can benefit students in engineering design practices. Int. J. Technol. Des. Educ. **27**, 107–129 (2017)

30. Kelley, T.R., Knowles, J.G.: A conceptual framework for integrated STEM education. Int. J. STEM Educ. **3**, 1–11 (2016)

31. English, L.D.: Learning while designing in a fourth-grade integrated STEM problem. Int. J. Technol. Des. Educ. **29**(5), 1011–1032 (2019)

32. Zhou, D., Gomez, R., Wright, N., Rittenbruch, M., Davis, J.: A design-led conceptual framework for developing school integrated STEM programs: the Australian context. Int. J. Technol. Des. Educ. **32**(1), 383–411 (2022)

33. Oxman, R.: The thinking eye: visual re-cognition in design emergence. Des. Stud. **23**(2), 135–164 (2002)

34. Suwa, M., Tversky, B.: What do architects and students perceive in their design sketches? A protocol analysis. Des. Stud. **18**(4), 385–403 (1997)

35. Acer, D.: Children and architecture: architectural design education for young children in Turkey. Child. Educ. **92**(2), 99–110 (2016)

36. Batic, J.: The field trip as part of spatial (architectural) design art classes. CEPS J. **1**(2), 73–86 (2011)

37. Seitamaa-Hakkarainen, P., Kangas, K., Raunio, A.M., Viilo, M.: Architecture project: city plan, home and users–children as architects. Procedia Soc. Behav. Sci. **45**, 21–31 (2012)

38. Fowler, S., Kennedy, J.P., Cutting, C., Gabriel, F., Leonard, S.N.: Self-determined learning in a virtual makerspace: a pathway to improving spatial reasoning for upper primary students. Int. J. Technol. Des. Educ. 1–22 (2023)

39. Bhaduri, S., Biddy, Q.L., Bush, J., Suresh, A., Sumner, T.: 3DnST: a framework towards understanding children's interaction with Tinkercad and enhancing spatial thinking skills. In: Interaction design and children, pp. 257–267 (2021)

40. Bhaduri, S., Van Horne, K., Sumner, T.: Designing an informal learning curriculum to develop 3D modeling knowledge and improve spatial thinking skills. In: Extended abstracts of the 2019 CHI conference on human factors in computing systems, pp. 1–8 (2019)

41. Khunyakari, R., Mehrotra, S., Chunawala, S., Natarajan, C.: Design and technology productions among middle school students: an Indian experience. Int. J. Technol. Des. Educ. **17**, 5–22 (2007)

42. Zhu, C., Klapwijk, R. M., Silva-Ordaz, M., Spandaw, J., De Vries, M.: Cognitive and embodied mapping of data: an examination of children's spatial thinking in data physicalization. Front. Educ. **8** (2023)

43. Chang, Y.: 3D-CAD effects on creative design performance of different spatial abilities students. J. Comput. Assist. Learn. **30**(5), 397–407 (2014)

44. Sutton, K., Williams, A.: Implications of spatial abilities on design thinking. In: Durling, D., Bousbaci, R., Chen, L, Gauthier, P., Poldma, T., Roworth-Stokes, S., Stolterman, E. (eds.), Design and complexity - DRS international conference 2010, 7–9 July, Montreal, Canada (2010)

45. Nazidizaji, S., Tomé, A., Regateiro, F.: Does the smartest designer design better? Effect of intelligence quotient on students' design skills in architectural design studio. Front. Architect. Res. **4**(4), 318–329 (2015)

46. Allen, A.D.: Complex spatial skills: the link between visualization and creativity. Creat. Res. J. **22**(3), 241–249 (2010)

47. Cho, J.Y.: An investigation of design studio performance in relation to creativity, spatial ability, and visual cognitive style. Think. Skills Creat. **23**, 67–78 (2017)

48. Dere, H.E., Kalelioglu, F.: The effects of using web-based 3D design environment on spatial visualisation and mental rotation abilities of secondary school students. Inform. Educ. **19**(3), 399–424 (2020)

49. Carbonell-Carrera, C., Saorin, J.L., Melián-Díaz, D., Hess-Medler, S.: Spatial orientation skill performance with a workshop based on green infrastructure in cities. ISPRS Int. J. Geo-Inform. **9**(4) (2020)

50. Lin, H.: Influence of design training and spatial solution strategies on spatial ability performance. Int. J. Technol. Des. Educ. **26**, 123–131 (2016)

51. Khooshabeh, P., Hegarty, M., Shipley, T.F.: Individual differences in mental rotation. Experim. Psychol. (2013)

52. Tzuriel, D., Egozi, G.: Gender differences in spatial ability of young children: the effects of training and processing strategies. Child Dev. **81**(5), 1417–1430 (2010)

53. Hegarty, M.: Ability and sex differences in spatial thinking: what does the mental rotation test really measure? Psychon. Bull. Rev. **25**, 1212–1219 (2018)

54. Hsi, S., Linn, M.C., Bell, J.E.: The role of spatial reasoning in engineering and the design of spatial instruction. J. Eng. Educ. **86**(2), 151–158 (1997)

55. Toth, A.J., Campbell, M.J.: Investigating sex differences, cognitive effort, strategy, and performance on a computerised version of the mental rotations test via eye tracking. Sci. Rep. **9**(1), 19430 (1997)

56. Bartlett, K.A., Camba, J.D.: Gender differences in spatial ability: a critical review. Educ. Psychol. Rev. **35**, 1–29 (2023)

57. Bartlett, K.A., Camba, J.: The role of a graphical interpretation factor in the assessment of Spatial Visualization: a critical analysis. Spat. Cogn. Comput. **23**(1), 1–30 (2023)

58. Caissie, A.F., Vigneau, F., Bors, D.A.: What does the Mental Rotation Test measure? An analysis of item difficulty and item characteristics. Open Psychol. J. **2**, 94–102 (2009)

59. Fisher, M.L., Meredith, T., Gray, M.: Sex differences in mental rotation ability are a consequence of procedure and artificiality of stimuli. Evol. Psychol. Sci. **4**, 124–133 (2018)

60. Ormand, C.J., et al.: Evaluating geoscience students' spatial thinking skills in a multi-institutional classroom study. J. Geosci. Educ. **62**(1), 146–154 (2014)

61. Uttal, D.H., McKee, K., Simms, N., Hegarty, M., Newcombe, N.S.: How can we best assess spatial skills? practical and conceptual challenges. J. Intell. **12**(1), 8 (2024)

62. Hambrick, D.Z., et al.: A test of the circumvention-of-limits hypothesis in scientific problem solving: the case of geological bedrock mapping. J. Exp. Psychol. Gen. **141**(3), 397 (2012)

63. Lawson, B.R.: Cognitive strategies in architectural design. Ergonomics **22**(1), 59–68 (1979)

64. Goldschmidt, G.: Linkographic evidence for concurrent divergent and convergent thinking in creative design. Creat. Res. J. **28**(2), 115–122 (2016)

65. Guilford, J.P.: The nature of human intelligence. McGraw-Hill, New York (1967)

66. Schut, A., Van Mechelen, M., Klapwijk, R.M., Gielen, M., de Vries, M.J.: Towards constructive design feedback dialogues: guiding peer and client feedback to stimulate children's creative thinking. Int. J. Technol. Des. Educ. 1–29 (2020)

67. Zhu, C., Klapwijk, R.M., Silva-Ordaz, M., Spandaw, J., de Vries, M.J.: Investigating the role of spatial thinking in children's design ideation through an open-ended design-by-analogy challenge. Int. J. Technol. Des. Educ. 1–30 (2024)

68. Torrance, E.P.: Torrance tests of creative thinking: norms technical manual. Ginn, Lexington, MA (1974)

69. Vandenberg, S.G., Kuse, A.R.: Mental rotations, a group test of three-dimensional spatial visualization. Percept. Mot. Skills **47**(2), 599–604 (1978)

70. Guay, R.: Purdue Spatial Visualization Test - Visualization of Rotations. W. Lafayette, IN. Purdue Research Foundation (1977)

71. Ramful, A., Lowrie, T., Logan, T.: Measurement of spatial ability: Construction and validation of the spatial reasoning instrument for middle school students. J. Psychoeduc. Assess. **35**(7), 709–727 (2017)

72. Harris, J., Newcombe, N.S., Hirsh-Pasek, K.: A new twist on studying the development of dynamic spatial transformations: mental paper folding in young children. Mind Brain Educ. **7**(1), 49–55 (2013)

73. Wilson, V., Harris, M.: Creating change? A review of the impact of design and technology in schools in England. J. Technol. Educ. **15**(2), 46–65 (2004)

74. Glück, J., Fitting, S.: Spatial strategy selection: interesting incremental information. Int. J. Test. **3**(3), 293–308 (2003)

75. Maresch, G.: Strategies for assessing spatial ability tasks. J. Geom. Graph. **18**(1), 125–132 (2014)

76. Adams, R.S., Atman, C.J.: Cognitive processes in iterative design behavior. In: FIE'99 frontiers in education. 29th annual frontiers in education conference. designing the future of science and engineering education. Conference proceedings, IEEE Cat. No. 99CH3701, vol. 1, pp. 11A6–13 (1999)

77. Looijenga, A., Klapwijk, R., de Vries, M.J.: The effect of iteration on the design performance of primary school children. Int. J. Technol. Des. Educ. **25**, 1–23 (2015)

78. National Research Council.: Learning to think spatially. The National Academies Press, Washington, DC (2006)

79. Herrington, A.J. Herrington, J.A.: What is an authentic learning environment?. In: Tomei, L.A. (ed.), Online and distance learning: concepts, methodologies, tools, and applications, pp. 68–77 (2007)

80. Herrington, J., Oliver, R.: An instructional design framework for authentic learning environments. Educ. Tech. Res. Dev. **48**(3), 23–48 (2000)

81. Kwon, O.N., Park, J.H., Park, J.S.: Cultivating divergent thinking in mathematics through an open-ended approach. Asia Pac. Educ. Rev. **7**, 51–61 (2006)

82. Kolodner, J.L., et al.: Problem-based learning meets case-based reasoning in the middle-school science classroom: putting learning by design (tm) into practice. J. Learn. Sci. **12**(4), 495–547 (2003)

83. Hmelo, C.E., Holton, D.L., Kolodner, J.L.: Designing to learn about complex systems. In Design education, pp. 247–298. Routledge (2000)

84. de Lavoir, S.V.P., den Otter, M.-J., de Vries, M., Barendsen, E.: Characterising structure-property reasoning within a chemical design challenge: green bubble soap. In: The 40th International Pupils' Attitudes Towards Technology Conference Proceedings (2023)

85. Stammes, H., Henze, I., Barendsen, E., de Vries, M.: Bringing design practices to chemistry classrooms: Studying teachers' pedagogical ideas in the context of a professional learning community. Int. J. Sci. Educ. **42**(4), 526–546 (2020)

86. Atit, K., et al.: Examining the relations between spatial skills and mathematical performance: a meta-analysis. Psychon. Bull. Rev. 699–720 (2022)

87. Hinze, S.R., Williamson, V.M., Shultz, M.J., Deslongchamps, G., Williamson, K.C., Rapp, D.N.: Spatial ability and learning from visualizations in STEM disciplines. In: Montello, D.R., Grossner, K., Janelle , D.G. (eds.) Space in mind: concepts for spatial learning and education, pp. 99–118. The MIT Press (2014)
88. Bilda, Z., Gero, J.S.: The impact of working memory limitations on the design process during conceptualization. Des. Stud. **28**(4), 343–367 (2007)
89. Klapwijk, R., van Doorn, F.: Contextmapping in primary design and technology education: a fruitful method to develop empathy for and insight in user needs. Int. J. Technol. Des. Educ. **25**(2), 151–167 (2015)
90. Smith, K.M.: Conditions influencing the development of design expertise: as identified in interior design student accounts. Des. Stud. **36**, 77–98 (2015)
91. Vossen, T.E., Henze, I., Rippe, R.C.A., Van Driel, J.H., de Vries, M.J.: Attitudes of secondary school students towards doing research and design activities. Int. J. Sci. Educ. **40**(13), 1629–1652 (2018)
92. Alias, M., Gray, D.E., Black, T.R.: Attitudes towards sketching and drawing and the relationship with spatial visualisation ability in engineering students. Int. Electron. J. **3**(3), 165–175 (2002)
93. Levin, L., Verner, I.M.: Fostering students' analytical thinking and applied mathematical skills through 3D design and printing. In: 2020 IEEE global engineering education conference (EDUCON), pp. 145–149. IEEE (2020)
94. Bicer, A., Nite, S.B., Capraro, R.M., Barroso, L.R., Capraro, M.M., Lee, Y.: Moving from STEM to STEAM: the effects of informal STEM learning on students' creativity and problem solving skills with 3D printing. In: 2017 IEEE frontiers in education conference (FIE), pp. 1–6. IEEE (2017)
95. Bufasi, E., et al.: Addressing the complexity of spatial teaching: a narrative review of barriers and enablers. Front. Educ. **9**, 1306189 (2024)
96. Uttal, D.H., et al.: The malleability of spatial skills: a meta-analysis of training studies. Psychol. Bull. **139**(2), 352–402 (2013)
97. Newcombe, N.S.: Picture this: increasing math and science learning by improving spatial thinking. Am. Educ. **34**(2), 29 (2010)

Divided Attention in Human-Robot Teaming: Assessing Performance in Large-Scale Interactive Virtual Environments

Xianshi Xie[1], Timothy P. McNamara[2], and Bobby Bodenheimer[3](✉)

[1] Uber, Sunnyvale, CA, USA

[2] Department of Psychology, Vanderbilt University, Nashville, TN, USA
t.mcnamara@vanderbilt.edu

[3] Department of Computer Science, Vanderbilt University, Nashville, TN, USA
bobby.bodenheimer@vanderbilt.edu

Abstract. This paper explores division of attention for people in human-robot teaming within immersive virtual environments (IVEs), focusing on search tasks where a supervisor oversees multiple robots distributed across various locations. We examine how spatial separation of robot teams affects supervisors' attention, performance, workload, and situational awareness. We investigate the cognitive impact of managing geographically divided teams. The study also considers how head movement and locomotion, activities involving crucial spatial cues, influence visual attention and spatial memory in complex tasks. Two experiments are conducted to analyze these effects in this applied setting, which could inform command and control structures for robot teams. The results of this research inform spatial attention for large-scale IVEs and could have broader implications for designing effective human-robot collaborations in various fields such as defense, search and rescue, and manufacturing.

Keyword: spatial attention · immersive virtual environments · human-robot teams

1 Introduction

Humans working with robots as a team are becoming increasingly important in many areas, such as search [17], search and rescue [23], manufacturing [11], and defense [3]. Immersive virtual environments (IVEs) provide an excellent platform to test human-robot teaming methods and assess people's cognitive capabilities, much as IVEs offer excellent capabilities to assess people's spatial learning [32]. This paper focuses on the effects of the spatial distribution of stimuli on attention during a demanding task scenario.

The particular task scenario is human-robot teaming, in which a human has to supervise a large robot team of multiple robots potentially distributed into multiple groups in the field. The goal is to investigate how people's attention is divided when the robot team is spatially separated. In such scenarios, the human supervisor may need to keep track of

M. Živković et al. (Eds.): Spatial Cognition 2024, LNAI 14756, pp. 114–127, 2024.
https://doi.org/10.1007/978-3-031-63115-3_8

multiple groups of robots; when the robot team is divided into multiple groups and the human supervisor has to locomote between the groups, we want to understand how the human's attention and performance are affected by this attention division and the need to locomote. Of course, it is easy to conjecture that a division of attention or a need to perform another task, such as locomotion, will adversely affect task performance. Still, the amount and nature in which performance is affected are unknown.

We chose the task to be a search task, that of searching suspicious objects. Searching suspicious targets is typical in some human-robot teaming scenarios [17]. In this task, human supervisors must supervise a robot team consisting of multiple robots, which may become geographically distributed and separated into multiple groups. Therefore, the human supervisors may have to divide their attention between the robot groups. McCormick et al. [20] showed that most evidence favored a unified model of spatial attention: attention modulation is confined to a single, indivisible focal region in the visual field. So, we ask how human attention is affected when teams are divided and how the spatial division affects performance. We want to determine how human performance, perceived workload [15], and situational awareness [10] are affected in the presence of large robot teams. Understanding the cognitive costs of the division of large robot teams in the field on a human supervisor has implications for the command-and-control structure of such teams.

More generally, the task we employ requires visual attention and spatial memory on the part of the human supervisor. While the relationship between spatial memory and visual attention has been explored in considerable depth (e.g., Woodman and Luck [31]), their relationship to larger factors such as complex search, head movement, and locomotion has not been studied. Some of these factors involve cues critical to spatial updating [21]. The present paper performs two in-depth experiments that explore this relationship in an applied scenario.

2 Background

Most people can coordinate and execute multiple tasks in a flexible manner [8], but training can improve performance [26]. However, performance can degrade when tasks become more cognitively demanding or the number of tasks increases. Human-robot teams typically require a human to perform multiple tasks when coordinating teams of robots, and thus, the modulation of attention is essential to successful human-robot interaction. In terms of the spatial distribution of teams and the attentional requirements involved, some evidence favors a unified model of spatial attention: attention modulation is confined to a single, indivisible focal region in the visual field [20]. Other work argues that observers can divide their attention to multiple spatial locations [1]. Jans et al. [18] suggested dividing attention might not be easily achieved by a naive human observer. Still, it is a skill that can be acquired only through training. This paper focuses on how people divide their attention into multiple groups of objects when placed under demanding visual task [30]. People can track multiple moving objects [22, 29], but concurrent tasks that demand attention reduce this tracking ability [29]. Self-motion, either active or passive, impairs the ability to track multiple objects [27].

Assessing the performance of human supervisors in human-robot teams has been done through a variety of means [6], and several salient abilities have been found, such as operator spatial ability and situational awareness. Likewise, operating in a human-robot team can involve mental effort on the part of the human supervisor; the mental workload is typically defined as the amount of cognitive resources needed to perform a task. Assessing the amount of effort involved in a task scenario and how it varies can be important in qualifying the characteristics of a task [13]. Mental workload can be measured through a variety of means; in this paper, we chose to measure it through a standardized self-report questionnaire, the NASA Task Load Index [14], which measures mental, physical, and temporal demand, performance, effort, and frustration level. Situational awareness is the perception and awareness of one's environments [9]. This paper will measure it by the 3D Situational Awareness Rating Technique, a standardized self-report [16]. The 3D SART is a questionnaire that participants rate on a seven-point scale (1 = low, 7 = high) for demands on attentional resources, supply of attentional resources, understanding of the situation, and overall situational awareness.

3 Experiment 1

Experiment 1 was designed to test how people divide their attention when they are placed in a demanding task scenario, i.e., supervising a large robot team in a typical search task scenario. In particular, we want to test how people divide their attention when the robot team is deployed differently.

For the search scenario, we employed an exhaustive search strategy. Exhaustive search guarantees that all participants search the entire space regardless of the random placement of the suspicious trashcans. The robots we modeled have a limited range of communication and sensing. Therefore, our robot team moved and searched side by side within a fixed range so that the robot team would cover all regions of the search area. The robots in the team must also be able to avoid the obstacles. For ground mobile robots, Latimer et al. [19] investigated the multi-robot coverage problem based on a single robot coverage algorithm, called the boustrophedon approach, which divides the planar area into regions called cells; simple back-and-forth motions cover each cell. Then, the whole area coverage is achieved when all cells are done. Multi-robot coverage uses the same planar cell-based approach. Multiple robots move side by side and sweep a cell simultaneously; robot teams are allocated among different cells. Robots within a team communicate and share information with one another while teams cover cells independently of each other. The advantage of path planning lies in a 2D configuration space for a team of n robots instead of planning in a $2n$ dimensional configuration space. Rekleitis et al. [24] extended this approach by allowing the robots to operate under the restriction that communication between two robots is available only when they can see each other. In this paper, we adopted the approach of these authors [19, 24] for our search strategy and adapted the general shape of searching space to a rectangular space. For all experiments, only small obstacles were randomly distributed over the entire area.

Automatic search through large areas is a complicated problem that could involve a large number of robots. There are at least four types of search strategy, e.g., hasty and heuristic search, constraining search, high probability region search, and exhaustive search [2]. We adopted an exhaustive search as our search strategy.

3.1 Method

We used twelve participants for this study, six males and six females, aged 18 to 30. All participants had normal or corrected to normal sight. No participants were familiar with the virtual environment or the experiment. All participants were compensated for their participation, $10 per hour. The Vanderbilt Institutional Review Board approved experimental protocols, and participants had the experiment explained and signed informed consent forms before participating.

This experiment consisted of the following scenario: a robot team, possibly distributed into two groups, searched a set of objects (trash cans) to see if any contained suspicious objects. A human observer was required to memorize the location of the trash cans that the robots designated as suspicious. The conditions of the experiment varied in how the robot team was distributed. In the first condition, the robot team acted together as a unit over a search area of 100×50 m. In the second condition, the robot team was broken into two groups over two search areas, each 50×50 m, searching simultaneously, with each area viewable from a single position where human observers had to turn their heads approximately $90°$. In the third condition, the robot team was broken into two groups over two search areas, each 50×50 m, searching simultaneously. Still, human observers had to locomote to view each area, as neither area was viewable from the view of the other one. These areas were approximately 30 m apart, and observers locomoted between them using a scaled translational gain of 15:1. We chose this gain because 15:1 is the lower bound of gain that allowed participants to walk a 30 m distance in the IVE within two seconds, which would allow them to have enough time switch from one robot group to the other. Within each area trash cans are laid out in a random (Poisson disk) manner. As described previously, the robot team conducted an exhaustive search of the area. For example, in the first condition, as shown in Fig. 1, eight robots started from the left half of the search area, 5 m apart from each other, moved and searched forward along straight reference paths, with a 0.5 m/s speed, until reaching the boundary of the search area. Then, the robot team moved to the other half of the search area and did the same search. The robots used simulated laser sensors to detect obstacles along the path and would pass around the obstacles once one was detected. All other experiments involving robots used the same search strategy. Along the path, when a suspicious object was found, the robot stopped and emitted a beeping sound for about 15 s to notify the observer. During this time, the trashcan changed color. There were six suspicious objects in each condition, three for each area in the second and third conditions. A trial consisted of one complete search, and after each trial, participants were asked to indicate which trash cans were suspicious. The design of the experiment was within subjects with gender and the order of conditions balanced. Five trials of each condition were experienced as a block.

In this experiment and the next, the Player/Stage robot framework was used to model, control, and simulate the actual robot behavior, running on an Ubuntu linux server platform [7, 12]. Player was used to set up robot servers; the Stage framework was also used to clone the trashcan environment. Player enabled us to use a built-in motion controller and simulated laser sensor of the robots. Then, in VR, we created one robot client (proxy) to control each robot by leveraging the built-in controller. The communication between robot servers and robot clients was established through a middle layer written in C++. The virtual environment was viewed through a full-color stereo NVIS nVisor SX60 head-mounted display HMD with 1280×1024 pixels resolution per eye.

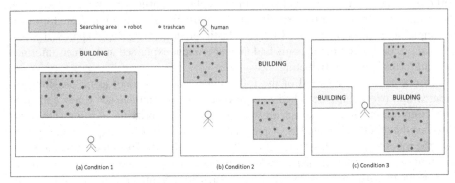

Fig. 1. Experiment 1: Search area layout of all three conditions. Human observers viewed at a distance of about 60 m from the center of the search area. In Condition 3, the center of the two areas is about 90 m apart.

We measured the correct selection proportion (CSP) of the trashcans and the latency. We also calculated a two-dimensional similarity between the correct configurations of the suspicious trashcans and the configurations of participants selection, using bidimensional regression [5, 28]. For the correspondence of the anchor points of the two configurations, we assumed the correct selected targets as pairs of points (e.g., we assume participants made the correct choice intentionally), iterated all possible per- mutations for incorrectly selected targets, and picked the configuration with highest r^2 (e.g., this measure indicates correspondence between two 2D configurations, ranged from 0 to 1; the higher, the more correspondence) among all permutations. After completing each condition, all participants also filled out NASA-TLX questionnaires for workload and 3D SART questionnaires for situational awareness.

3.2 Results

Figure 2 shows that the average ratio of correctly selected trashcans to the total number (i.e., correct selection proportion, CSP) in the first condition (the Standing & 1Group, S1G) is about 0.9, indicating participants incorrectly selected about 0.6 trashcans on average (less than 1) out of the array of six target trashcans. In the second and third conditions (Standing & 2Group, S2G, and Locomotion & 2Group, L2G, respectively), the ratio of correctly selected trashcans to the total is about 0.76 and 0.72, respectively, which means participants incorrectly selected about 1.5 trashcans on average. A one-way repeated measures ANOVA showed a main effect on these ratios of condition, $F(2,22) = 11.33, p < 0.001$.

A post-hoc analysis using a paired sample t-test with Bonferroni correction showed a significant difference between the S1G and S2G conditions, $t(11) = 3.45, p = 0.005$, and between the S1G and L2G conditions, $t(11) = 3.95, p = 0.002$. Thus, separating the teams decreased people's performance (by over a factor of 2), but the addition of locomotion did not further affect the performance. There were no significant differences in the amount of time it took participants to select the configurations of objects.

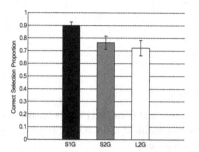

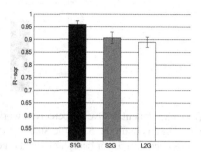

Fig. 2. Experiment 1: The correct selection ratio across conditions. S1G stands for the Standing & 1Group condition; S2G, the Standing & 2Groups condition; and L2G, the Locomotion & 2Groups condition. Error bars show standard errors of the mean.

Fig. 3. Experiment 1: The r^2 across conditions. S1G stands for the Standing & 1Group condition; S2G, the Standing & 2Groups condition; and L2G, the Locomotion & 2Groups condition. Error bars show standard errors of the mean.

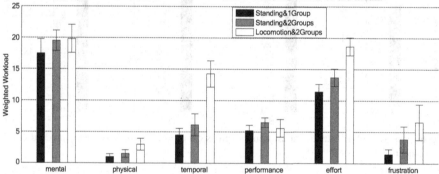

Fig. 4. Experiment 1: Perceived workload across conditions. Error bars show standard errors of the mean.

The r^2 resulting from the bi-dimensional regression analysis, which showed the degree of correspondence between the two configurations ranged from 0 to 1 after translation, scaling, and rotation, was analyzed in a one-way repeated measures ANOVA.

The result showed a main effect of the conditions, $F(2,22) = 8.07$, $p = 0.002$. A post-hoc paired sample t-test with Bonferroni correction showed a difference between the S1G condition and the S2G condition ($t(11) = 2.9$, $p = 0.01$) and between the S1G condition and the L2G condition ($t(11) = 4.01$, $p = 0.002$). From Fig. 3, the S1G condition had higher r^2 ($r^2 = 0.96$) than the S2G ($r^2 = 0.91$) and the L2G ($r^2 = 0.89$) condition. Note that Figs. 2 and 3 show the same pattern even though they are different dependent measures. Because they are different measures, they are not redundant with one another but rather indicate convergent validation.

For perceived workload, we see there was an increasing trend of overall workload from Condition 1 (S1G condition) to Condition 3 (L2G condition), which have means

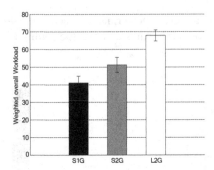

Fig. 5. Experiment 1: Overall perceived workload across conditions. S1G stands for the Standing & 1Group condition; S2G, the Standing & 2Groups condition; and L2G, the Locomotion & 2Groups condition. Error bars show standard errors of the mean.

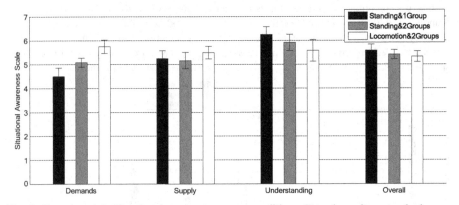

Fig. 6. Experiment 1: Situational awareness across conditions. Error bars show standard errors of the mean.

41.09, 51.23, and 67.90 (on a scale of 100), respectively (Fig. 5). An ANOVA showed the three conditions are significantly different ($F(2,22) = 16.94, p < 0.001$). A post-hoc paired-sample t-test with Bonferroni correction between the S2G and L2G conditions shows a significant difference ($t(11) = 3.76, p = 0.003$). This result was expected since participants not only had to divide their attention but also had to walk back and forth to keep track of both robot teams. The overall workload increased by 32%.

Six factors contributed to the overall perceived workload: mental demand, physical demand, temporal demand, performance, effort, and frustration. Each factor was analyzed using ANOVA analysis across conditions. The results that showed significance were in physical demand ($F(2,22) = 3.66, p = 0.04$), temporal demand ($F(2,22) = 11.89, p < 0.001$) and effort ($F(2,22) = 9.95, p < 0.001$). From Fig. 4 we see all these three factors were higher in the L2G condition than the other two conditions.

For situational awareness (Fig. 6), a within-subjects ANOVA showed that there was a significant effect of demand ($F(2,22) = 6.48, p = 0.006$) but no effect of supply, understanding, or overall situational awareness. A post-hoc paired-sample t-test with

Bonferroni correction on the demand factor revealed a significant difference between the S1G and L2G conditions ($t(11) = 2.9164, p = 0.01$).

3.3 Analysis

Separating the areas of search decreased performance (mis-selection almost doubled) and increased the perceived workload. The reason is that participants have to keep track of both areas simultaneously and have to move their heads back and forth frequently, which causes more disruption during their memorization process. Note that the total number of robots, trashcans, and suspicious trashcans are identical across the conditions. Another observation is that locomotion did not appear to decrease the performance further but did increase the perceived workload dramatically. We conjecture there are several reasons why the performance did not decrease further. First, the locomotion interval was quite short, i.e., less than a couple of seconds are required to move from one area to the other. Second, the search process of robots last about two minutes, which was long enough for participants to scan and rehearse the locations of the suspicious trashcans found by the robots. Third, participants were able to see most of the search area at the standing or observing location, which facilitated their employing a simple strategy of memorizing the suspicious trashcans. For example, some participants reported they divided the trashcans into groups by the proximity of the trashcans, which helped select suspicious trashcans since participants stood at roughly the same location with the same viewpoint to choose those trashcans. However, the perceived workload increased from the S2G condition to the L2G condition, especially in temporal demand, effort, and physical demand. The results suggest that participants have to work harder in the locomotion condition to achieve the same level of performance as the S2G condition. The BDR measure is consistent with the CSP measure, which means that the geometry similarity between the selection configuration and the correct configuration is also decreased by the robot team separation.

4 Experiment 2

In the previous experiment, for the S2G condition, the robot team split into two groups searching for two areas, and the two groups were located at some distance away (see Fig. 1b). Participants had to turn 90 degrees to see one of the two areas. However, in the first condition, participants only need to turn small angles to see the search area. Thus, two factors were inherently confounded in this condition: the separation of the robot team, which divides attention, and the need to use head movements, which has the entire team out of the field of view at one time. In this experiment, we controlled for these factors independently.

4.1 Method

The method and protocols were similar to Experiment 1, with the difference being that we have only two conditions. The first condition is the same as the first condition of Experiment 1. However, in the second condition, the two search areas are located side by side, and participants have the same field of view of the whole search area for both conditions. Thus, the only difference between the two conditions is the robot team splits into two groups in the second condition. Thus, the difference in the S2G condition between Experiment 1 and 2 is that the two areas in Experiment 1 were far apart. Participants had to make a larger head turn angle (around 90°) to see the two areas in the S2G condition but only make a small head turn angle (around 50°) to see the whole area in Experiment 2. In this experiment, we used 12 participants, six male and six female. The experiment was order and gender balanced.

4.2 Results

The correct selection proportion (CSP) had a mean of 0.87 in the S1G condition and 0.79 in the S2G condition (Fig. 8), which indicates that participants mis-selected 0.78 trashcans out of 6 suspicious trashcans in the S1G condition, and mis-selected 1.26 trashcans in the S2G condition. A one-way repeated measures ANOVA showed a main effect of the separation, $F(1,11) = 7.86$, $p = 0.017$. Therefore, separating the robot team into two groups, even with the same field of view of the search area, significantly decreased participants' performance by mis-selecting about 0.5 more trashcans, around 61% more. There was a gender effect in this experiment, $F(1,10) = 9.20$, $p = 0.013$. Male participants did better, with a CSP of 0.95 and 0.86 for each condition, respectively, than female participants, with a CSP of 0.80 and 0.72 for each condition, respectively. It took about 33 s on average to complete the selection, and there was no significance between the two conditions in terms of duration in completing the task. There was no effect of the order in which the participants did the conditions (Fig. 7).

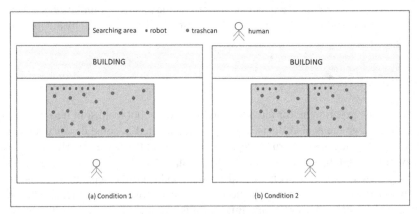

Fig. 7. Experiment 2: The search area layout for the two conditions. The participant viewed the robots from a distance of about 60m from the center of the search area(s).

For the NASA-TLX questions, an ANOVA analysis showed a main effect on overall weighted workload, $F(1,11) = 15.0$, $p = 0.0026$, which shows participants perceived over- all workload was higher in the S2G condition than in that of the S1G condition

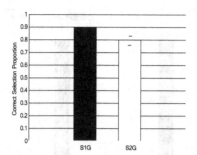
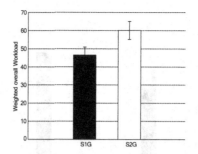

Fig. 8. Experiment 2: The correct selection ratio across conditions. Error bars show standard errors of the mean.

Fig. 9. Experiment 2: Overall perceived workload across conditions. Error bars show standard errors of the mean.

(Fig. 9). For the six factors, only mental demand was significant, $F(1,11) = 10.2, p = 0.008$. Please see Fig. 10 for details.

For situational awareness, there was a main effect of demand on attentional resources, $F(1,11) = 7.3, p = 0.021$, which showed that the S2G condition required much more demand placed on participants' attentional resources by completing the task than that of the S1G condition. Results showed no effect on the factors of supply, understanding, or overall situational awareness. Please see Fig. 11 for more details.

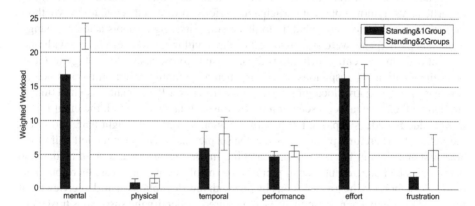

Fig. 10. Experiment 2: Perceived workload components across conditions. Error bars show standard errors of the mean.

We also did a mixed model two-by-two ANOVA for Experiments 1 and 2, Experiment (between) × Condition (within), in which we dropped the L2G condition of Experiment 2. We found a main effect of condition, $F(1,22) = 19.72, p < 0.001$, but no effect on the experiment. Therefore, the separation of the team decreased performance, not the turning angle.

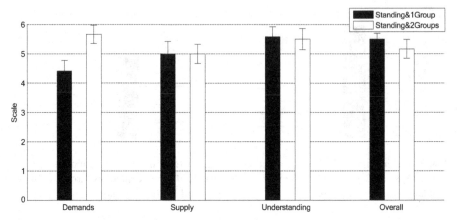

Fig. 11. Experiment 2: Situational awareness measures across conditions. Error bars show standard errors of the mean.

5 Discussion

Participants memorized more than 70% of the suspicious trashcans in both experiments. In the S1G condition of Experiments 1 and 2, the CSPs are around 90%. Although eight robots and the large search area with 20 trashcans inside initially seemed overwhelming to participants, it turned out that participants performed well in this condition. We think there are several factors contributing to this result. First, eight robots acted as a single team, and participants were able to see all of them within the field of view or with only a slight head movement, which allowed participants to use a simple strategy to memorize the locations of suspicious trashcans, such as grouping several trashcans nearby and learning the relative locations between the trashcans. Participants also had time to strengthen their mental representation of the trashcan layout. Second, the eight robots moved side by side, swept the left half of the area, moved to the right half, and swept the right half. Therefore, participants saw the suspicious trashcans in the left half of the area first and then in the right half. Searching in the two subareas was in tandem, so participants had concurrent mental representations of the two subareas; therefore, participants memorized the trashcans one by one with few disruptions. Third, the viewpoint remained the same when participants were required to identify the suspicious trashcans. However, the separation of the robot team, not the amount of head movement, decreased participants' performance. When the robot team split into two groups and the search area divided into two areas, participants had to maintain two mental representations of the trashcan layouts. During the search, participants had to switch between the two mental representations, which were different from the S1G condition, with the two concurrent mental representations. Therefore, the frequent switch between the two mental representations requires more effort and resources than the concurrent processing of the two mental representations. The switching process increased the difficulty level of the task and perceived workload.

In Experiment 1, we noticed that locomotion might be a second factor affecting the performance because there is a trend (not significant) that participants performed worse in the locomotion condition than in the standing condition. In addition, locomotion increased the perceived workload significantly. A possible reason for this trend is that locomotion makes the task more rushed and thus increases the temporal demand. Similarly, some evidence shows that self-motion, either active or passive, impairs the ability of multiple-object tracking [27], and people employ a common mechanism to track changes both to the locations of moving objects around them and to keep track of their positions. In our task scenarios, participants needed to maintain their orientation and keep track of their locations during the locomotion, which demands attention.

Thus, they suffered a cognitive cost due to locomotion, regardless of occlusion or not. We noticed that although the task was more demanding than Experiments 1 and 2, participants still had comparable performance, with around 75% CSP, which means participants could still do the task even when the search time was reduced to about 1 min.

The finding regarding head movement is interesting and could promote future work. Recent work in navigation in IVEs with HMDs has shown gender-based differences in head movement in navigational performance [33]. Likewise, males tend to rely more on distal cues that allow for the development of survey knowledge when navigating [4, 25]. Since HMDs are still heavy and unergonomic, understanding the conditions under which head movement is a beneficial component of a task may be useful as VR training and education become more prevalent.

6 Conclusion

This paper presented two experiments demonstrating how people flexibly attend to demanding tasks in large immersive virtual environments. Specifically, we investigated the scenarios where a person is working with a large robot team consisting of multiple robots that are potentially distributed into multiple groups in a large space, all visible through either head turning or with some locomotion. Our findings indicated that performance degraded when the robot team was separated but that the spatial separation of the team did not matter. The separation of the robot team decreased the supervisor's performance, increased the perceived workload, and increased the demand on attentional resources. The amount of head movement was not a significant factor in performance. There was some suggestion that locomotion led to a decrease in performance. However, this was not a significant finding in our study, and further work would be needed to investigate this effect. The findings of these experiments show that there is a primary cognitive cost to robot team separation and locomotion, which could have design implications for human-robot and human-agent teams in IVEs and real-world conditions.

Acknowledgments. The authors would like to thank Qiufeng Lin for help throughout. This material is based upon work supported by the National Science Foundation under grants 1526448 and 1763966.

References

1. Adamo, M., Pun, C., Pratt, J., Ferber, S.: Your divided attention, please! the maintenance of multiple attentional control sets over distinct regions in space. Cognition **107**(1), 295–303 (2008)
2. Adams, J.A., Cooper, J.L., Goodrich, M.A., Humphrey, C., Quigley, M.G.B., Morse, B.S.: Byuhcmi technical report: Camera-equipped mini UAVS for wilderness search support: task analysis and lessons from field trials (2007)
3. Adams, J.A., Scholtz, J., Sciarretta, A.: Human-robot teaming challenges for the military and first response. Ann. Rev. Control Robot. Auton. Syst. **7**, 1 (2024)
4. Andersen, N.E., Dahmani, L., Konishi, K., Bohbot, V.D.: Eye tracking, strategies, and sex differences in virtual navigation. Neurobiol. Learn. Mem. **97**(1), 81–89 (2012)
5. Carbon, C.-C.: Bidimregression: bidimensional regression modeling using r. J. Statist. Software Code Snippets **52**, 1(3), 1–11 (2013)
6. Chen, J.Y.C., Barnes, M.J.: Human-agent teaming for multirobot control: a review of human factors issues. IEEE Trans. Hum.-Mach. Syst. **44**(1), 13–29 (2014)
7. Collett, T.H., Macdonald, B.A., Gerkey, B.P.: Player 2.0: Toward a practical robot programming framework. In: Proceedings of the australasian conference on robotics and automation (ACRA 2005), p. 145 (2005)
8. Drigas, A., Karyotaki, M.: Attentional control and other executive functions. Int. J. Emerg. Technol. Learn. (Online) **12**, 3, 219 (2017)
9. Endsley, M.R.: Measurement of situation awareness in dynamic systems. Hum. Fact. J. Hum. Fact. Ergon. Soc. **37**, 1, 65–84 (1995)
10. Endsley, M.R.: Direct measurement of situation awareness: validity and use of SAGAT. In: Endsley, M.R., Garland, D.J (eds.) Situation awareness analysis and measurement. Lawrence Erlbaum Associates, Mahwah, NJ, USA (2000)
11. Faccio, M., et al.: Human factors in cobot era: a review of modern production systems features. J. Intell. Manuf. **34**(1), 85–106 (2023)
12. Gerkey, B., Vaughan, R.T., Howard, A.:. The player/stage project: tools for multi-robot and distributed sensor systems. In: Proceedings of the 11th international conference on advanced robotics, vol. 1. 317–323 (2003)
13. Harriott, C.E., Buford, G.L., Adams, J.A., Zhang, T.: Mental workload and task performance in peer-based human-robot teams. J. Hum.-Robot Interact. **4**(2), 61–96 (2015)
14. Hart, S., Staveland, L.: Development of NASA-TLX (Task Load Index): results of empirical and theoretical research. In: Hancock, P., Meshkati, N. (eds.) Human Mental Workload, pp. 139–183. North Holland Press, Amsterdam (1988)
15. Hart, S.G., Stavenland, L.E.: Development of NASA-TLX (Task Load Index): results of empirical and theoretical research. In: Hancock, P.A., Meshkati, N. (eds.) Human Mental Workload, Elsevier, Chapter 7, 139–183 (1988)
16. Humphrey, C.M., Henk, C., Sewell, G., Williams, B.W., Adams, J.A.: Assessing the scalability of a multiple robot interface. In: Proceedings of the 2nd ACM/IEEE international conference on human-robot interaction. New York, NY, USA, 239–246 (2007)
17. Humphrey, Curtis M., Adams, J.A.: Robotic tasks for chemical, biological, radiological, nuclear and explosive incident response. Adv. Robot. **23**, 1217–1232 (2009)
18. Jans, B., Peters, J.C., de Weerd, P.: Visual spatial attention to multiple locations at once: the jury is still out. Psychol. Rev. **117**(2), 637 (2010)
19. Latimer, D.I., Srinivasa, S., Lee-Shue, V., Sonne, S., Choset, H., Hurst, A.: Towards sensor based coverage with robot teams. In: IEEE international conference on robotics and automation, 2002. Proceedings. ICRA 2002, vol. 1. 961–967 (2002)

20. McCormick, P., Klein, R., Johnston, S.: Splitting versus sharing focal attention: comment on castiello and umiltà (1992). J. Exp. Psychol. Hum. Percept. Perform. **24**(1), 350–357 (1998)
21. Newman, P.M., McNamara, T.P.: Integration of visual landmark cues in spatial memory. Psychol. Res. **86**(5), 1636–1654 (2022)
22. Pylyshyn, Z.W., Storm, R.W.: Tracking multiple independent targets: evidence for a parallel tracking mechanism. Spat. Vis. **3**(3), 179–197 (1988)
23. Queralta, J.P., et al.: Collaborative multi-robot search and rescue: planning, coordination, perception, and active vision. IEEE Access **8**, 191617–191643 (2020)
24. Rekleitis, I., Lee-Shue, V., New, A.P., Choset, H.: Limited communication, multi-robot team based coverage. In: 2004 IEEE international conference on robotics and automation, 2004. Proceedings. ICRA 2004, vol. 4. 3462–3468 (2004)
25. Sandstrom, N.J., Kaufman, J., Huettel, S.A.: Males and females use different distal cues in a virtual environment navigation task. Cogn. Brain Res. **6**, 351–360 (1998)
26. Strobach, T., Frensch, P.A., Schubert, T.: Video game practice optimizes executive control skills in dual-task and task switching situations. Acta Physiol. (Oxf) **140**(1), 13–24 (2012)
27. Thomas, L.E., Seiffert, A.E.: Self-motion impairs multiple-object tracking. Cognition **117**(1), 80–86 (2010)
28. Tobler, W.R.: Bidimensional regression. Geograph. Anal. **26**, 3, 187–212 (1994)
29. Tombu, M., Seiffert, A.E.: Attentional costs in multiple-object tracking. Cognition **108**(1), 1–25 (2008)
30. Wickens, C.D., Carswell, C.M.: Information processing. Hand-book of human factors and ergonomics, pp. 114–158 (2021)
31. Woodman, G.F., Luck, S.J.: Serial deployment of attention during visual search. J. Exper. Psychol. Hum. Percept. Perform. **29**(1), 121 (2003)
32. Zhao, J., et al.: Desktop versus immersive virtual environments: effects on spatial learning. Spat. Cogn. Comput. **20**(4), 328–363 (2020)
33. Zhao, Y., Gagnon, H., Stefanucci, J.K., Creem-Regehr, S.H., Bodenheimer, B.: Eye gaze reveals gender differences in mixed reality navigation. In: CHI EA 2024: Extended Abstract of the 2024 CHI Confrence on Human Factors in Computing Systems. In Review

Early Childhood

'Bear Hunt' Sparks Change: Using Lesson Study to Integrate Spatial Thinking in Early Childhood Design Education

Rohit Mishra[✉] and Remke M. Klapwijk

Delft University of Technology, Delft 2628 CJ, The Netherlands
r.mishra@tudelft.nl

Abstract. Developing spatial ability in early childhood is crucial, but not all children are naturally drawn to spatial activities like construction. For those with different play preferences, integrating design and construction tasks with storybooks will engage them more, tapping into their problem-solving interests. Despite the central role of storytelling in early childhood education, it's relatively new for teachers to use stories to engage children in spatialized design assignments. This study addresses this gap by implementing a Lesson Study approach in six Irish junior and senior infant classrooms from two schools with ten teachers. Qualitative data from classrooms and teacher discussions reveal positive outcomes: teachers altered their lesson strategies, gained insights into their students' spatial thinking, improved spatial design assignment development, and enhanced selfefficacy in conducting spatialized lessons. These outcomes underscore the efficacy of Lesson Study for professional development in early childhood spatial education.

Keywords: Spatial Thinking · Lesson Study · Design Instruction · Early childhood · Teacher Professional Development

1 Introduction

As children construct towers with blocks, navigate mazes, and create small-world prototypes with toys in early childhood classrooms, they are unknowingly developing a crucial skill - spatial thinking. Spatial thinking, involving an awareness of space and the ability to solve problems mentally [34], serves as a gateway for young learners to attain advanced educational and occupational credentials in Science, Technology, Engineering and Math (STEM) [41]. Recent meta-analysis [44] emphasizes the importance of early spatial intervention, pointing out that the malleability of spatial skills is more pronounced in younger children (average effect size, Hedges's g = 0.96), surpassing the average effect size (g = 0.47) observed in the general population [38]. This underscores the substantial impact of early spatial intervention.

Using construction activities to develop spatial thinking is well-researched, and professional development strategies have been developed for teachers [18, 28]. However, not all children exhibit motivation for spatial activities such as construction.

M. Živković et al. (Eds.): Spatial Cognition 2024, LNAI 14756, pp. 131–146, 2024.
https://doi.org/10.1007/978-3-031-63115-3_9

In a qualitative study in two Dutch schools, Sonneveld et al. [31] noticed that some children do not like construction. They prefer role play and enjoy pretending with toys like small dolls or chairs. To engage children with diverse play preferences, incorporating design and construction assignments tied to storybooks could be more effective [31]. Fleer [13] observes that many children enjoy solving problems for characters in a story. Fleer conjectures that the use of stories aids children in visualizing the context of their creations. Informed by Klapwijk & Stables [24], the inherent inclination of young children to create and shape their world is a fundamental aspect of human nature. Researchers at the University of Surrey in the UK[1] and the University of Canberra in Australia[2] have compiled a list of stories suitable for teaching STEM lessons with a focus on spatial skills. Despite this, there is a gap in research regarding using such stories for creating design and construction assignments aimed at enhancing children's spatial skills.

Storytelling plays a crucial role in early childhood classrooms, and teachers frequently use storytelling in their classrooms [13]. However, it is new for most teachers to utilize stories to engage children in open-ended design tasks. In design education, students quickly learn to generate satisfactory solutions to ill-defined problems [8]. Open-ended design tasks are multifaceted challenges that involve students in exploring diverse solutions, resulting in a wide range of ideas for teachers to interpret [42]. Therefore, teachers need to know how to identify a spatialized design challenge from a story and formulate it in a manner that allows for multiple solutions to provide pupils with open-ended design tasks. They need to be able to notice the presence of spatial thinking during design and understand how different levels of spatial thinking and creativity will influence their pupils' performance. Finally, teachers need to know how they can best support each child. If we want teachers to include spatial design tasks using stories as a starting point to engage more children in spatial activities, we need sound professional development strategies.

Shulman [32] emphasizes the critical importance of teachers possessing various types of knowledge that serve as the foundation for their decision-making in practice. This foundational knowledge includes content knowledge, pedagogical content knowledge, and general pedagogical knowledge, forming interconnected strands that act as intellectual scaffolding for guiding teachers in their professional endeavors. According to a meta-analysis by Sims & Wood [32], key elements essential for successful Professional Development (PD) are: 1) Cultivating teachers' insights, 2) Motivation for change, 3) Development of teaching techniques, and 4) Integration of these changes into teachers' everyday practice. The Japanese Lesson Study approach taken in our study embodies these key elements, keeping teachers' various types of knowledge in mind. Lesson Study has been proven effective in deepening teachers' knowledge of their own pupils [29], enhancing teaching practices [9, 40], and increasing teacher self-efficacy [35].

In response to the need for supporting teachers in integrating and facilitating open-ended spatialized design activities for pupils aged four to six, a PD program was developed in this study in cooperation with a teacher training institute in Ireland. The PD

---

[1] https://earlymaths.org/spatial-books/.

[2] https://elsaprogram.com.au/wp-content/uploads/2022/02/STEM-Booklist_Publishing-040 518.pdf.

program included an introductory workshop on fostering spatial thinking. It adopted two cycles of the Lesson Study in each classroom, with a final meeting of the teachers' group to facilitate knowledge sharing. The primary goal is to cultivate teachers' abilities to develop a design assignment related to a children's storybook that would provide children opportunities to use spatial reasoning in problem-solving and design. This paper outlines the setup and outcomes of the PD program in terms of teachers' knowledge of their own pupils, enhancing spatial teaching practices, and self-efficacy in teaching spatial tasks.

2 Literature Review

2.1 Professional Development (PD) Strategies for Teachers

Although various countries worldwide have introduced design and technology education, the focus on developing spatial thinking through open-ended design assignments is relatively new [31, 45–47], emphasizing the necessity to understand better how effective PD can take place. Strategies for PD may vary, including workshops and courses, Instructional Coaching (defined as 'an observation and feedback cycle in an ongoing instructional situation' [21]), Teacher Learning Communities (described as 'teacher learning in a community setting where teachers convene over time to reconsider their existing beliefs and practices' [6]), and Lesson Study (characterized as 'observation of live classroom lessons by a group of teachers who collect data on teaching and learning and collaboratively analyze it' [27].

Although workshop and course-based PD help educators acquire new knowledge, the transition to applying this knowledge in practice often poses a significant challenge. Instructional coaching, a personalized support system aimed at fostering individual growth for educators, is often hindered by its high cost and the potential lack of peer support, given its predominantly one-on-one nature. Therefore, our focus in this paper is on PD strategies that are especially effective in supporting teachers in integrating new teaching techniques into their everyday practice. International review studies [10, 20, 43] underline Lesson Study's impact on teachers' knowledge, behavior, attitudes, and its influence on student learning. Lesson Study, originating from Japan, is a structured process focusing on studying pupils' learning in a live educational setting. Through collaborative efforts, teachers investigate the cognitive processes involved in their students' learning. At its core, Lesson Study involves the observation of live classroom lessons by a group of teachers who collect data on teaching and learning and collaboratively analyze the findings to drive instructional improvements [9, 26, 27]. Its collaborative nature fosters sustainable professional growth among teachers, with evidence suggesting significant shifts in teachers' learning patterns [40]. In Lesson Study's cyclical approach, a particular focus on 'case pupils' [9], representing certain learner groups based on their ability or other characteristics is present. All Lesson Study phases involve these case students, which might be a promising strategy to teach teachers to identify and support diverse spatial thinking processes present in a classroom. Lesson Study continuously challenges teachers to anticipate their students' responses and design lessons to cater to the needs of different ability groups, ideally guided by a facilitator or 'knowledgeable other' [36]. Lesson studies, characterized by five 'big ideas' [11, 15]: 1) encourage teachers to understand students 2) blend personal and external knowledge 3) research their own practices, 4) engage in collaborative discussions 5) follow a cyclical approach for ongoing improvement.

The outcomes of lesson studies include heightened pedagogical content knowledge [9, 16, 30], improved knowledge of students [29], improved learning patterns of teachers [40], and increase in teachers' self-efficacy [7, 35]. The 'knowledgeable other' role is critical in guiding teachers to incorporate novel pedagogical content. External experts, sometimes also serving as facilitators, bring new knowledge to the group of teachers. For topics unfamiliar to teacher participants, instructional workshops are common to transfer new pedagogical content knowledge before the teachers start designing the research lesson [2, 11]. The collaborative and reflective approach allows teachers to integrate external knowledge into their expertise [11, 36].

Lesson Study's effectiveness in developing various aspects of teachers' professional capacity makes it a valuable form of PD for spatialized design assignments. Earlier, Hawes et al. [18] employed Lesson Study to train teachers in spatializing the math curriculum, and this year-long intervention resulted in enhanced spatial thinking in four to seven-year-olds, including improved 2D mental rotation and visual-spatial geometry. Our study focuses on using Lesson Study to integrate design assignments based on children's storybooks, emphasizing spatial thinking through hands-on activities. The following section will delve into the specific pedagogical content knowledge relevant to our target group.

2.2 Pedagogical Content Knowledge (PCK) for Teachers of Early-Childhood Classrooms in Developing Spatial Design Activities

Many aspects of spatial thinking are integral to children's natural development at home and school. For instance, Yang et al. [44], in a meta-analysis on the effectiveness of spatial skills training in early years, suggested that hands-on exploration, visual prompts, use of spatial language, and spatial gesture training significantly foster young children's spatial skills. Additionally, Cartmill et al. [4], and Kisa et al. [23] recommended that teachers employ spatial language and gestures in their classroom instruction, which proved beneficial in developing spatial thinking for learners aged four to seven years. Research has indicated that construction activities are valuable in the early classroom. Uttal et al. [38], and Hawes et al. [19] suggest various spatially demanding activities, such as copying block constructions, designing number lines with block play, and creating walking paths in the classroom. These tasks should be goal-oriented and guided play to capture the attention of young children. Our focus is on a different type of task: the children are provided with a story and asked to solve a design challenge related to this story. For teachers, it is important to understand how to develop open-ended design tasks that allow for multiple solutions [24] and how prototyping - using sketches and materials to develop solutions - works in the classroom [25].

Design thinking and spatial thinking are related to each other. For example, in a recent study Zhu et al. [45], 37 children aged 11–12 engaged in guided design activity to create tangible data visualizations.

The Irish teachers in our study are not used to such open-ended design tasks, and it is also new for them to foster spatial thinking during design activities. Providing teachers with (external) information and tools to foster spatial thinking is important in this Lesson Study.

2.3 Lesson Study Structure Integrating the PCK Needs of Teachers

A 1.5-h workshop served as a foundational overview, emphasizing the importance of fostering spatial thinking through Science, Technology, Engineering, Art, and Math (STEAM) activities and hands-on design and construction experiences. The content of the workshop included five spatial tools to foster spatial thinking in early childhood classrooms: (1) use of spatial language, (2) use of gestures, (3) use of manipulatives with a "think then do!" approach, facilitating thinking before doing a task, (4) story-based design tasks with construction toys, and finally, (5) the Lesson Study approach to assess case pupils' learning. These elements were regarded as initial steps to incorporate spatial thinking through story-based design in early childhood education, aligning with the key points of the Aistear Framework. In Ireland, Aistear is the curriculum framework (2009) for children aged from birth to six years old. In addition, to provide examples and background information on these five spatial tools the Spatial Reasoning Toolkit developed by The Early Childhood Mathematics Group (ECMG)[3] was introduced [14]. The Toolkit includes posters, videos, guidance, and a learning trajectory from birth to age Seven, showcasing trajectories for key aspects of spatial reasoning: Movement and navigation, Shape properties, and Shape composition and construction. Table 1 below provides an overview of the Lesson Study structure used in our study.

Table 1. The Lesson Study structure for each classroom adapted from Dudley [9]

1	Work shadowing by first author to know the current practices in classrooms.	1 Day
2	Workshop on fostering spatial thinking	1.5 hours
3	Developing the research lesson and selecting case pupils	1 hour
4	Implementing lesson (First Lesson Study Cycle) – including observation and short interview with case pupils	1 hour
5	Post-lesson discussion of teachers and facilitator	30 minutes
6	Second Lesson Study Cycle, implementing adapted lesson	1 hour
7	Second post-lesson discussion	30 minutes
8	Final meeting of 10 participants sharing their learning from Lesson Study	1 hour

Our Central Research Question Is: "What are the outcomes of a Lesson Study approach in supporting Irish early childhood teachers with respect to deepening their knowledge of their pupils, enhancing teaching practices, and impacting teacher self-efficacy, specifically in relation to spatial reasoning during story-based design activities?".

---

[3] available at: https://earlymaths.org/spatial-reasoning.

3 Method Section

In this first design round, a design-based research approach [39] was applied using a case-study approach to gain in-depth knowledge of the Lesson Study approach. A key element in design research is the creation of an educational innovation that considers the complexity of the context. In our case, we studied the learning processes and outcomes of the participant teachers.

3.1 Participants

Ten teachers from two different Irish schools actively engaged in the Lesson Study cycles. In School A, where the region's schools are relatively small, only two teachers, along with the facilitator (first author), formed a Lesson Study group. Meanwhile, in School B, teachers also worked in pairs, attending the spatial thinking workshop together. During the final post-lesson discussion, all ten teachers convened online for reflection. School A was chosen for practical reasons to assess the effectiveness of the lesson study cycle in facilitating teacher learning in a small school setup. This paper analyzes only the dialogue and classroom instructions from School A: one teacher for junior infants and another for senior infants. Both participating teachers are female, with the senior infant teacher having over ten years of teaching experience and the other with five years of experience. Pseudonyms, Ms. Cassidy, and Ms. Nally have been used in this paper to protect the anonymity of the teachers of Junior Infants and Senior Infants, respectively. Both classrooms had 20 children in each with an age range of four to six years old.

3.2 Data Collection

Data collection occurred during both the facilitated teacher meetings and in classrooms. All teacher meetings and the workshop were audio-recorded. Discussion on lesson plans and adaptations after the post-lesson discussion were collected. The first author and the teachers observed the classroom example pupils and took photos of the intermediate and final designs by the pupils. The first author transcribed the audio data from all sessions. Pupil A, Pupil B, and Pupil C are three case students chosen by classroom teachers, each representing – an expert, developing, and beginner in spatial skills. In identifying the case children as experts, developing, or beginners in spatial skills, teachers relied primarily on their professional judgment. This process was informed by teachers' experiences and beliefs about their pupils and their understanding of what defines spatial design capabilities.

4 Analysis

Kager and colleagues [22] present a conceptual model of continuous professional development through Lesson Study, which systematically explores outcomes and contributing elements for successful PD. Outcomes are defined across various levels: satisfaction and acceptance of PD represent the first level, with subsequent levels focusing on enhancement in knowledge, beliefs, attitudes (level two), change in teaching practice (level three), organizational changes (level four), and sustained enhanced student performance (final level). Our analysis concentrated on outcomes at the second and third levels of the conceptual model. Although the literature on lesson studies presents nuanced categorizations of learning outcomes, we focused on three themes: teachers deepening their knowledge of their pupils [29], enhanced teaching practices and instruction [9, 40], and teacher's self-efficacy [35]. During the analysis phase, the first and second authors conducted three rounds of categorization, selecting, and comparing sections of conversation highlighting key themes. While we identified more than three categories, we reported on three main themes for our preliminary analysis, focusing on school A. A third researcher external to the research coded the episodes from teachers in school A, with only one episode coded differently. After discussion, it became evident that two themes were intertwined in this episode.

5 Results

The preliminary results of two teachers at School A will be presented here. Both teachers collaboratively developed a lesson plan during the first series of meetings and devised a design assignment related to the story narrating Michael Rosen's "We're Going on a Bear Hunt." Each research lesson began with the teacher narrating the story with attention to spatial words and using gestures. Next, pupils were tasked with creating a trap to capture the bear, initiating with sketching out their ideas and then building it with materials.

Below, we will delineate the episodes representative of the learning that occurred for the following three themes: 1) Deepening Teachers' Knowledge of Pupils, 2) Change in Teaching Practices and instructional strategies, and 3) Increased Teacher Self-Efficacy. These teachers worked in pairs, with one observing the pupils and how they reacted to the activities during the research lesson.

5.1 Planning the Research Lesson

Before detailing the learning outcomes for teachers, the subsequent planning episode, occurring immediately after the workshop (Step 3 of Table 1), illustrates the evolving thought processes of the two teachers on seeking suitable storybooks and creatively transforming narratives into spatially challenging design tasks.

Episode 1: Post-workshop discussion during lesson planning between teachers

1. *Ms. Cassidy: So, we go with the story (We're Going on a Bear Hunt Book by Michael Rosen).*
2. *Ms. Nally: Yeah, and then implemented during Aistear. We were doing Little Red Riding Hood, and the brief was to trap the wolves for construction. So, that's what the construction points are doing.*
3. *Ms. Cassidy: Very good.*
4. *Ms. Nally: But, like in the home corner, they're making food for grandma at the kitchen.*
5. *Ms. Cassidy: Lovely.*

6. *Ms. Nally: Yeah, and then in arts and crafts, they were designing a map for Little Red Riding Hood's return to grandma's house or to get to the wolf, or whatever they come up with themselves.*
7. *Ms. Cassidy: So, let's just take a story or fairy tale or something, and then we put the brief for each station.*
8. *Ms. Nally: Yeah.*
9. *Ms. Nally: I don't know what story? Is it the Bear Hunt that you're thinking of (to choose)?*
10. *Ms. Cassidy: Yeah, we can use it.*
11. *Ms. Nally: Because there is a lot of [spatial] language when you're reading it with them. That's your language, and you are getting it explicitly, and the gestures acted out and stuff.*
12. *Ms. Cassidy: The language is there, yeah, and getting them to the movements. So, you're given the language of through, over, under. So now we have to give them a task based on the story.*
13. *Ms. Nally: Yeah, a practical one that they solve with design, you know, by making. Can you do something with the cave?*
14. *Ms. Cassidy: Yeah, trap the bear in the cave?*
15. *Ms. Nally: Or the cave is dark, so light up the cave? Or is it hard for junior infant, I suppose.*
16. *Ms. Cassidy: Yeah.*
17. *Ms. Nally: Is there a forest?*
18. *Ms. Cassidy: Yeah, there's a forest, grass, water, and mud that they could pick maybe. So, they pick an area and trap the bear in each different area? So they could decide the area and come up with a trap?*
19. *Ms. Nally: Yeah! A trap based on five different designs.*
20. *Ms. Cassidy: Or even if they were given that freedom kind of which one [area] they choose.*
21. *Ms. Nally: Oh yeah, let them decide the way to set a trap.*

In this episode, Ms. Cassidy selects a book for a design task, aligning objectives with Ms. Nally to incorporate spatial language. Ms. Nally reflects on past projects, emphasizing spatial literacy activities within classroom corners. They deliberate the potential of the chosen book, considering its rich spatial language. Practical challenges, like trapping the bear or illuminating the cave, are discussed, tailored to student developmental levels, as Ms. Nally realized through discussion that "lighting up a cave" would be a difficult task for her pupils. This collaborative process underscores careful planning, highlighting teachers' ability to create effective design tasks based on their knowledge of the class. Finally, pupils were tasked with constructing a bear trap using various materials. Materials included Duplo blocks, Lego, and more. At the end of the lesson, pupils shared their designs, which provided an opportunity for the use of spatial language and gestures. The above episode showcases the value of teacher-developed assignments, leveraging their contextual understanding and enhancing the learning experience for their pupils.

5.2 Teachers' Knowledge of Their Pupils

After formulating the lesson plan, the teachers proceeded to implement it in their respective classrooms, with one teacher actively teaching while the other observed the identified case pupils using an observation sheet. The observation sheet included five tools aimed at fostering spatial thinking in the early childhood classroom, derived from the workshop, enabling teachers to observe students' use of spatial language, gestures, and progress in design tasks. The observing teacher utilized this sheet for post-lesson discussions. In the subsequent post-lesson discussion detailed below, the teachers engaged in a dialogue, focusing on their observations of the case students, with special attention given to their pupils labeled as C, the pupils they expected to have a beginner-level spatial ability.

1. *Ms. Cassidy: Pupil C [beginner spatial ability], I was really surprised of what he came up with. He was actually fantastic.*
2. *Ms. Nally: The imagination is [fantastic]*
3. *Ms. Cassidy: Yeah*
4. *Ms. Nally: I was just wondering if he'd be on task or not, that was my [Pupil] C.*
5. *Ms. Cassidy: and that was the same with my child C. It is the same thing that I didn't think that he'd do but it is actually the interest was there.*
6. *Ms. Nally: Yeah [interest] of what they were doing was there*
7. *Ms. Cassidy: Yeah and then that kept them focused. just that he had an interest in the topic and then he use his imagination and that kept him on task*
8. *Ms. Nally: Yes absolutely*
9. *Ms. Cassidy: But it is so interesting that these children that we picked that they will go off task were the ones that actually did best*
10. *Ms. Nally: Surprised us.*
11. *Ms. Cassidy: Yeah absolutely.*

Both teachers express surprise at the performance of a case pupil C, initially placed in the beginner spatial ability group, noting the pupil's remarkable imagination. They had doubted whether beginner pupils, denoted by the letter C, would stay on task but were pleasantly surprised to find them motivated and engaged. The senior infant teacher links this motivation to the pupil's interest in the topic and ability to utilize imagination, which ultimately led to their success. This discovery challenges the teachers' initial expectations and highlights the importance of recognizing and nurturing students' individual qualities. Despite initial reservations, the story framework effectively engaged beginner spatial ability pupils. While expert and developing spatial ability pupils performed as expected, one junior infant pupil perceived as expert spatial ability by teachers initially showed limited spatial language use, possibly due to shyness during observation. However, upon repeating the lesson, the pupil demonstrated satisfactory spatial language skills.

In the following episode, Ms. Cassidy, who observed the lesson, shared insights from her interview with Pupil C during his design task during the post-lesson discussion.

1. *Ms. Cassidy: When I went over to him [pupil C], he said, "I'm drawing a map," and he said, "I did instructions for it."*
2. *Ms. Nally: Yeah.*
3. *Ms. Cassidy: So, he was even talking about his design [sketch]. He was using a lot of spatial language, like that the trap will go over the bear when you put it out there; it will be a cage, he will get squashed down, these [areas] have to be covered, this is the way to slam [the cage gate], and he was moving on the different parts.*
4. *Ms. Nally: Yeah! There was a part at the top that was moving up and down.*

5. *Ms. Cassidy: Yeah, so he was very [involved]. Then he explained the wheel that they spin and these are the cutters, and when the bear breaks out… so we really had a lot of thoughts on what he was doing, and then he was talking about the wacker goes up and down, up and down, then he put a camera on it as well, and it goes in there and talks about … he [actually] made a bear.*
6. *Ms. Nally: And he showed us.*
7. *Ms. Cassidy: Yeah, and how the bear would go in here, and then they get trapped.*
8. *Ms. Cassidy: Yeah, so really engaged, really good spatial thinking, and that was your pupil C.*
9. *Ms. Nally: Yeah! [Laughs with surprise].*

Here the observing teacher shares insights she got from interviewing beginner ability Pupil C, who had surprised both teachers with technical details and spatial language use while describing his design. Sentence 3 captures the specific instance where Pupil C not only described his design but used advanced technical terms like "instructions" and considered the design as a "map," showcasing some understanding of the spatial elements. Sentences 3–6 show how Pupil C adeptly used spatial language to describe the intricate details of the trap's functionality, showcasing a higher level of spatial thinking than perceived by the teachers as he relates the form to the function of the design. This discussion between teachers shows how Lesson Study can deepen teachers' knowledge of pupils and they are also learning how a child can bring spatial language and technical understanding to a design process. The combination of having to predict how the case pupil will behave, observing the actual behavior, using during-class interviews and a reflection (Step 5, Table 1.) together led to deepened knowledge of pupils during a spatialized design assignment.

5.3 Change in Teaching Practices and Instructional Strategies for Spatialized Design Activities

In the post-lesson discussion following the initial lessons in both Junior and Senior Infant classes (Step 5, Table 1), teachers reflect on various activities. The selected episode captures the point where teachers begin to recognizing the instructional potential inherent in utilizing sketches as reference points.

1. *Ms. Nally: I think I'm gonna leave my sketches with my children so that they can refer to it whenever they're building their traps.*
2. *Ms. Cassidy: yeah!*
3. *Ms. Nally: Because I just thought last time some of them were talking about their sketch and wanted to show me their design, but I had already collected it.*
4. *Ms. Cassidy: Yeah.*
5. *Ms. Nally: So, I think I will leave it on their table to refer back.*
6. *Ms. Cassidy: Yeah, the sketches were good just for that you know they think then do they definitely…*
7. *Ms. Nally: yeah, …give them time to think about what they want their design to look like.*
8. *Ms. Cassidy: yeah.*

In this exchange, Ms. Nally initiates the conversation by expressing her intention to leave sketches with the children based on her reflection from the previous lesson (sentences 1 to 5). Ms. Cassidy agrees, emphasizing the importance of allowing children time to think about their designs (sentence 7). The teachers collectively recognize the value of sketches in aiding children's memory and understanding of their design tasks. Ms. Cassidy agreed and added that leaving sketches with children also matches one of the five tools they learned during the workshop, which is "think then do" (sentence 6).

The teachers implement this change in a later lesson (step 6, Table 1). In the post-lesson discussion (step 7, Table 1) that follows the implementation of leaving sketches with the children, teachers explore the impact of this instructional shift on pupils' use of spatial reasoning.

1. *Ms. Cassidy: Sketch!*
2. *Ms. Nally: Yeah, sketch. I left the sketches on their tables, and some of them used it in their actual design, which I thought was good.*
3. *Ms. Cassidy: A lot of them did. And some built on top of their sketches, putting some pieces on it.*
4. *Ms. Nally: Some referred back to their sketch, saying, "This is the tree I built."*
5. *Ms. Cassidy: Yeah! They were describing it.*
6. *Ms. Nally: Yeah! That's why I think it was a good change as well.*
7. *Ms. Cassidy: I think it was interesting. One of them, the child had drawn like a door and a keyhole and a key, and then she had, when she showed me everything, yeah, in her Lego she had the keyhole and key and all.*
8. *Ms. Nally: Yeah, yeah, so they were referring back afterwards. I didn't take up the sketches last time, but I think it was a good idea to leave them with them.*
9. *Ms. Cassidy: And Child C in your room, he was saying, "Look, they look exactly the same," you know.*
10. *Ms. Nally: Yeah.*
11. *Ms. Cassidy: And he kept going back to the sketch.*
12. *Ms. Nally: Yeah, it's so interesting to see.*

In this exchange, Ms. Cassidy initiates the conversation with the exclamation "Sketch!" as an important change in their lesson plan. Ms. Nally observed that leaving the sketches on the children's tables had a beneficial impact on their engagement and design process (sentences 2 to 6). An anecdote about Pupil C highlights the significance of providing students with a reference point, as he recognizes the similarity between his sketch and the actual design (sentences 9 to 11). This example about sketches shows how, through Lesson Study, teachers are changing instructional strategies for spatialized design activities. Although the practice of keeping sketches available during 3D proto-typing is generally known in design and technology education [12], these teachers who are novices in design education discover the value of this practice and are motivated to implement this change. Teachers implemented additional changes, such as excluding open-ended materials like straws, toilet rolls, and cardboard from junior infant classes. Instead, they emphasized the use of Legos, as they found cutting and folding activities challenging for younger pupils. They showcased various designs made by pupils, encouraging the use of spatial language. Following the Lesson Study, they discussed adjustments to pupil grouping, aiming for natural collaboration, such as during Aistear time. Ms. Nally utilized cosmic yoga from YouTube to engage students, with a focus on spatial language.

5.4 Increased Teacher Self-Efficacy

In the subsequent teacher dialogue, during the final reflection on the Lesson Study cycle (Step 8, Table 1.), Ms. Nally and Ms. Cassidy reflect on their learning. They offer insights into the teachers' increasing confidence and efficacy in integrating spatial thinking into their regular teaching practices.

1. *Ms. Nally: Overall, we are more aware of the importance of developing spatial thinking, especially in the early years of school. We've also become aware of the link between a deep understanding of spatial language in the early years and spatial ability later in life.*
2. *Ms. Cassidy: We realized the importance of using gestures to enable a deeper understanding of spatial language. We've also recognized the significance of using a story stimulus to help embed memory, particularly episodic memories. We find the spatial thinking development toolkit useful as it shows opportunities to include spatial language in daily teaching. Going forward, we plan to use the five spatial tools for fostering spatial thinking in lessons. This involves incorporating more design and make tasks in our Aistear (early childhood framework in Ireland) and linking them to a story stimulus. We will continue to use gestures in our teaching practice, as it is something we already do frequently, whether giving instructions for teaching letters or numbers, showing direction, or engaging in poem songs and nursery rhymes. We'll also continue to reflect on the children's learning.*

In the final reflection on their learning, Ms. Nally and Ms. Cassidy highlight their increased awareness of spatial thinking's importance, emphasizing its connection to later-life spatial ability. They recognize the value of gestures and story stimuli, planning to integrate these elements into lessons. Miss Cassidy mentions, "We've also realized the importance of using a story stimulus to help embed memory," indicating their intention to utilize these techniques. As they discuss plans to incorporate design tasks within the Aistear framework, this conversation reveals their growing confidence in integrating "five spatial tools" given to them during the workshop, offering insights into their efficacy in seamlessly incorporating spatial thinking into regular teaching practices.

6 Discussion and Conclusion

Our aim was to study the outcomes of a Lesson Study approach and how it may deepen teachers' knowledge of their pupils, teaching practices, and its impact on teacher self-efficacy, specifically in relation to spatial reasoning during story-based design activities.

Preliminary results indicate that teacher learning occurred on each of the three selected themes. Teachers' knowledge of their pupils increased. Through case pupil selection, teachers gained insights into beginner pupils' spatial thinking, challenging pre-conceived notions and prompting shifts in beliefs about beginner pupils' abilities and how to engage such pupils in design tasks. Furthermore, enhancement in teaching practices was evident. Teachers' use of sketches to aid memory and communication aligned with workshop themes for effective spatial learning. Teachers also implemented five spatial tools, including spatial language and gesturing, and through reflection, changed and improved these teaching and instruction practices. Although these improvements are subjective, driven by teachers' experiences, imagination, and their interpretations of external information, they are a worthwhile step toward spatialized design assignments. The results also show the teachers' creativity in crafting assignments from storybooks, showcasing their ability to include design-based spatialized activities. Although the episodes on developing design assignments do not conclusively determine if teachers acquired new skills or already possessed them, the focus on spatial elements within storytelling is evidently new. Finally, some increase in teacher self-efficacy has been noted in the final meeting of teachers. Their plans to continue with spatialized design assignments and the use of five tools for fostering spatial thinking indicate possible sustainability. Compared to earlier PDs done in spatial thinking integration in classrooms [18, 28], one of the biggest barriers has been the time constraints from the side of participating teachers in long interventions for incorporating required instructional changes for fostering spatial thinking [3]. Our preliminary results suggest that the lesson study processes implemented in our study may motivate teachers to integrate spatial thinking into their classrooms while they are still working on their curriculum.

Further analysis of outcomes in school B is ongoing, which will provide additional insights. Future investigations will also delve into mechanisms of lesson study contributing to these outcomes, such as the workshop's alignment with participants' personal knowledge and the effectiveness of five spatial tools and observations in enhancing teacher self-efficacy. While the generalizability of findings requires careful consideration, they lay a foundation for empowering teachers to effectively support children with diverse spatial abilities in early childhood education.

Acknowledgments. This research is a component of SellSTEM (Spatially Enhanced Learning Linked to STEM), a Marie Skłodowska-Curie Innovative Training Network dedicated to exploring the significance of spatial ability in STEM learning. It has been financially supported by the European Union's Horizon 2020 research and innovation program under the Marie Skłodowska-Curie grant agreement (grant number 956124). We express our gratitude to the Monahan Education Center in Ireland for their support throughout this research. We thank Caiwei Zhu for her contributions to data analysis and Estefania Gamarra Burga for her valuable comments. Special thanks go to the participating teachers, students, and school principals from both schools.

Disclosure of Interests. The authors declare that the research was conducted in the absence of any commercial or financial relationships that could be construed as a potential conflict of interest.

References

1. Bates, K.E., et al.: Practitioners' perspectives on spatial reasoning in educational practice from birth to 7 years. Bri. J. Educ. Psychol. **93**(2), 571–590 (2023). (Wiley). https://doi.org/10.1111/bjep.12579

2. Benedict, A.E., Brownell, M., Bettini, E., Sohn, H.: Learning together: teachers' evolving understanding of coordinated word study instruction within an RTI framework. Teach. Educ. Spec. Educ. **44**(2), 134–159 (2021). https://doi.org/10.1177/0888406420930686

3. Bufasi, E., et al.: Addressing the complexity of spatial teaching: a narrative review of barriers and enablers. Front. Educ. **9**, 1306189 (2024). Frontiers Media SA. https://doi.org/10.3389/feduc.2024.1306189

4. Cartmill, E.A., Pruden, S.M., Levine, S.C., Goldin-Meadow, S.: The Role of Parent Gesture in Children's Spatial Language Development (2010)

5. Cerbin, W., Kopp, B.: Lesson study as a model for building pedagogical knowledge and improving teaching. Int. J. Teach. Learn. High. Educ. **18**(3), 250–257 (2006)

6. Chow, A.W.K.: Teacher learning communities: the landscape of subject leadership. Int. J. Educ. Manage. **30**(2), 287–307 (2016). https://doi.org/10.1108/IJEM-07-2014-0105

7. Chong, W.H., Kong, C.A.: Teacher collaborative learning and teacher self-efficacy: the case of lesson study. J. Exper. Educ. **80**(3), 263–283 (2012). https://doi.org/10.1080/00220973.2011.596854

8. Cross, N.: Designerly ways of knowing. Springer (2006). https://doi.org/10.1016/014269 4X(82)90040-0

9. Dudley, P.: Teacher learning in Lesson Study: What interaction-level discourse analysis revealed about how teachers utilised imagination, tacit knowledge of teaching and fresh evidence of pupils learning, to develop practice knowledge and so enhance their pupils' learning. Teach. Teach. Educ. **34**, 107–121 (2013)

10. de Vries, S., Roorda, G., van Veen, K.: The effectiveness and practicability of Lesson Study in the Dutch educational context (2017)

11. de Vries, S., Goei, S.L., Verhoef, N.: Basisboek Lesson Study in de lerarenopleiding. Boom uitgevers. (in Dutch) (2023)

12. English, L.D.: Learning while designing in a fourth-grade integrated STEM problem. Int. J Technol. Des. Educ. **29**, 1011–1032 (2019). https://doi.org/10.1007/s10798-018-9482-z

13. Fleer, M.: The genesis of design: learning about design, learning through design to learning design in play. Int. J. Technol. Des. Educ. **32**, 1441–1468 (2022). https://doi.org/10.1007/s10 798-021-09670-w

14. Gifford, S., et al.: Spatial Reasoning in early childhood (2022). https://doi.org/10.31234/osf.io/jnwpu

15. Goei, S.L., et al.: Online lesson study: Virtual teaming in a new normal. Int. J. Lesson Learn. Stud. **10**(2), 217–229 (2021). https://doi.org/10.1108/IJLLS-09-2020-0078

16. Goh, R., Fang, Y.: A tale of two schools: curriculum deliberation and school-level orientation in transforming knowledge through lesson study. Int. J. Lesson Learn. Stud. **12**(2), 166–178 (2023). https://doi.org/10.1108/IJLLS-02-2022-0026

17. Gilligan-Lee, K.A., et al.: Spatial Thinking in Practice: a snapshot of teacher's spatial activity use in the early years' classroom (2022). https://doi.org/10.31234/osf.io/zqc2x

18. Hawes, Z., Moss, J., Caswell, B., Naqvi, S., MacKinnon, S.: Enhancing children's spatial and numerical skills through a dynamic spatial approach to early geometry instruction: effects of a 32-week intervention. Cogn. Instruct. **35**(3), 236–264 (2017). Informa UK Limited. https://doi.org/10.1080/07370008.2017.1323902

19. Hawes, Z.C.K., Gilligan-Lee, K.A., Mix, K.S.: Effects of spatial training on mathematics performance: a meta-analysis. Develop. Psychol, **58**(1), 112–137 (2022). https://doi.org/10.1037/dev0001281

20. Huang, R., Shimizu, Y.: Improving teaching, developing teachers and teacher educators, and linking theory and practice through lesson study in mathematics: an international perspective. ZDM Math. Educ. **48**, 393–409 (2016). https://doi.org/10.1007/s11858-016-0795-7

21. Joyce, B.R., Showers, B.: Transfer of training: the contribution of "coaching." J. Educ. **163**, 163–172 (1981)

22. Kager, K., Mynott, J.P., Vock, M.: A conceptual model for teachers' continuous professional development through lesson study: capturing inputs, processes, and outcomes. Int. J. Educ. Res. Open **5**, 100272 (2023). https://doi.org/10.1016/j.ijedro.2023.100272

23. Kısa, Y.D., Aktan-Erciyes, A., Turan, E., Göksun, T.: Parental use of spatial language and gestures in early childhood. Bri. J. Develop. Psychol. **37**(2), 149–167 (2019). https://doi.org/10.1111/bjdp.12263

24. Klapwijk, R., Stables, K.: Design learning: pedagogic strategies that enable learners to develop their design capability. In: Gill, D., Irving-Bell, D., McLain, M., Wooff, D. (eds.) Bloomsbury handbook of technology education, pp. 271–289. Bloomsbury Publishing (2023)

25. Klapwijk, R., Rodewijk, N.: Purposeful prototyping through a discussion game in primary education. In: Proceedings of Fabler Netherlands 2018. Maker education in the Netherlands–state of play and lessons for the future, pp. 50–61 (2018)

26. Lewis, C., Perry, R., Murata, A.: How Should Research Contribute to Instructional Improvement? The Case of Lesson Study. Educ. Res. 35(3), 3–14 (2006). https://doi.org/10.3102/0013189X035003003

27. Lewis, C., Perry, R., Murata, A.: How should research contribute to instructional improvement? The case of lesson study. Educ. Res. **35**(3), 3–14 (2006). https://doi.org/10.3102/0013189X035003003

28. Lowrie, T., Logan, T., Ramful, A.: Visuospatial training improves elementary students' mathematics performance. Bri. J. Educ. Psychol. **87**(2), 170–186 (2017). https://doi.org/10.1111/bjep.12142

29. Moss, J., Hawes, Z., Naqvi, S., Caswell, B.. Adapting Japanese Lesson Study to enhance the teaching and learning of geometry and spatial reasoning in early years classrooms: a case study. In: ZDM, vol. 47, Issue 3, pp. 377–390. Springer Science and Business Media LLC (2015). https://doi.org/10.1007/s11858-015-0679-2

30. Schipper, T.M., Goei, S.L., de Vries, S.: Dealing with the complexity of adaptive teaching through collaborative teacher professional development. In: Maulana, R., Helms-Lorenz, M., Klassen, R.M. (eds.) Effective Teaching Around the World: Theoretical, Empirical, Methodological and Practical Insights, pp. 707–722. Springer International Publishing, Cham (2023). https://doi.org/10.1007/978-3-031-31678-4_32

31. Sonneveld, L.T., Klapwijk, R.M., Stappers, P.J.: Constructing and storytelling: accommodating different play orientations in learning spatial thinking. Front. Educ. **9**(1307951), 1–22. Article 1307951 (2024). https://doi.org/10.3389/feduc.2024.1307951

32. Shulman, L.S.: Those who understand: knowledge growth in teaching. Educ. Res. **15**, 4–14 (1986). https://doi.org/10.3102/0013189X015002004

33. Sims, S., Fletcher-Wood, H.: Identifying the characteristics of effective teacher professional development: a critical review. School Effect. School Improve. **32**(1), 47–63 (2021). https://doi.org/10.1080/09243453.2020.1772841

34. Schneider, J., McGrew, K.: The Cattell-Horn-Carroll theory of cognitive abilities. In: Flanagan, D., McDonough, E. (eds.), Contemporary intellectual assessment: theories, tests, and issues, pp. 73–163. The Guilford Press (2018)

35. Schipper, T., Goei, S.L., de Vries, S., van Veen, K.: Developing teachers' self-efficacy and adaptive teaching behaviour through lesson study. Int. J. Educ. Res. **88**, 109–120 (2018). https://doi.org/10.1016/j.ijer.2018.01.011

36. Takahashi, A., McDougal, T.: Collaborative lesson research: maximizing the impact of lesson study. ZDM Math. Educ. **48**, 513–526 (2016). https://doi.org/10.1007/s11858-015-0752-x

37. Tian, J., Ren, K., Newcombe, N.S., Weinraub, M., Vandell, D.L., Gunderson, E. A.: Tracing the origins of the STEM gender gap: the contribution of childhood spatial skills. Develop. Sci. **26**(2), e13302 (2023). https://doi.org/10.1111/desc.13302

38. Uttal, D.H., et al.: The malleability of spatial skills: A meta-analysis of training studies. Psychol. Bull. **139**(2), 352–402 (2013). https://doi.org/10.1037/a0028446

39. Van den Akker, J., Gravemeijer, K., McKenney, S., Nieveen, N. (eds.): Educational design research, 1st edn. Routledge (2006). https://doi.org/10.4324/9780203088364
40. Vermunt, J.D., Vrikki, M., van Halem, N., Warwick, P., Mercer, N.: The impact of Lesson Study professional development on the quality of teacher learning. In: Teaching and teacher education, vol. 81, pp. 61–73. Elsevier BV (2019). https://doi.org/10.1016/j.tate.2019.02.009
41. Wai, J., Lubinski, D., Benbow, C.P.: Spatial ability for STEM domains: aligning over 50 years of cumulative psychological knowledge solidifies its importance. J. Educ. Psychol. **101**(4), 817–835 (2009). https://doi.org/10.1037/a0016127
42. Watkins, J., et al.: Data-based conjectures for supporting responsive teaching in engineering design with elementary teachers. Sci. Educ. **102**(3), 548–570 (2018)
43. Xu, H., Pedder, D.: Lesson Study an international review of the research. In: Dudley, P. (ed.), Lesson Study: professional learning for our time, pp. 29e58. Routledge, London (2015)
44. Yang, W., Liu, H., Chen, N., Xu, P., Lin, X.: Is early spatial skills training effective? ameta-analysis. Front. Psychol. **11**, 1938 (2020). https://doi.org/10.3389/fpsyg.2020.01938
45. Zhu, C., Klapwijk, R.M., Silva-Ordaz, M., Spandaw, J., De Vries, M.J.: Cognitive and embodied mapping of data: an examination of children's spatial thinking in data physicalization. Front. Educ. **8**, 1308117 (2023). https://doi.org/10.3389/feduc.2023.1308117
46. Zhu, C., Klapwijk, R., Silva-Ordaz, M., Spandaw, J., de Vries, M.J.: Investigating the role of spatial thinking in children's design ideation through an open-ended design-by-analogy challenge. Int. J. Technol. Des. Educ. 1–30 (2024)
47. Zhu, C., et al.: Fostering spatial ability development in and for authentic STEM learning. Front. Educ. **8**, 1138607 (2023). https://doi.org/10.3389/feduc.2023.1138607

Author Index

M. Živković et al. (Eds.): Spatial Cognition 2024, LNAI 14756, p. 147, 2024.
https://doi.org/10.1007/978-3-031-63115-3

Printed in the United States
by Baker & Taylor Publisher Services